Dear Angie–

Mandate of an Apostl
To impress upon you with how complete
you are in Christ, because of God's doing!

1 COR 4:1 The Mirror
This is how one should regard us (so called,
Apostles): we are the under-rowers of Captain
Christ; responsible for the engine room as it
were!
We are entrusted with the administration of The
Mysteries of God.
The unveiling of the mystery of the gospel of
mankind's association in Christ is the driving
force of The Church.

Jer 33:3 The Message
"This is God's Message, the God who made earth,
made it livable and lasting, known
everywhere as God: 'Call to Me and I will
answer you. I'll tell you marvelous and
wonderous things that you could never
figure out on your own.'"

Loved

A 90 day journey
into the heart of God

Liz Wright and Gretchen Rodriguez

ISBN-13: 978-1-8381648-5-0

Cover design: Iain Gutteridge
Publisher: Liz Wright Ministries Ltd.

Contents

Acknowledgments

Gretchen Rodriguez. Your heart of love for our King pours through you as eloquent, supernatural speech. You are a rare jewel, a woman of great love and purity of heart. You are a gift in this world. Thank you for pouring yourself into helping me articulate and steward well the revelations Jesus has entrusted me with for His beloved people. Each heart's response you have composed will change lives as Jesus draws everyone through them and into His heart.

Mary King. Your beautiful, pure heart and incredible creative ability in editing, formatting, and writing which all flow from a depth of love for Jesus, never ceases to bless my heart as I see His love and wisdom in you every day. Thank you for all you do as we create with Jesus together.

Susan Wright. For always hearing God! For always being there. Your love and loyalty, your courage, and your belief in everyone you love is life-changing. Without you, this book wouldn't have come into being. You are a woman of great beauty. Thank you for what you pour into us all, constantly. You are a treasure to so many of us privileged to call you friend and sister.

My beloved husband, daughter, friends, and family. You are my treasures in life. I am rich because of you.

To our Intercessors, Founders, and International Mentoring Community family. I love doing life with you. I am truly blessed. Together forever.

Dedication

To Jesus,

My heart is Yours.

The Invitation

The most important moment in life is when we experience the love of God. This is what changes everything. As you immerse yourself in each revelation and encounter I share within the pages of this book, Jesus will speak to you and draw you deeply into His heart. Every word is for you.

You are about to embark on the most important discovery of your life; God is calling you deeper into knowing Him. He wants you to live from the experience of your union with Him, convinced of His love for you. Day by day, as you journey deeper, His love will become your core strength. From here, you will become unshakeable, face to face, heart-to-heart, one with God.

From this new depth of intimacy, you will soar with newfound confidence in His faithfulness, goodness, and sovereignty, and of your own immense value. Your heart will feel exhilarated, fulfilled, and utterly content. Your own passionate love for Jesus will be reignited. Rest and gratitude will become two foundations of your inner life. Your true self will emerge, shining with the beauty and power of a heart kissed awake and flooded with divine virtue. You will love because you have been loved. This is the moment everything changes. This is your moment.

With all my love,

Liz Wright

Day 1

Healing Oil

For I am the Lord who heals you.

Exodus 15:26 NKJV

Every need of your beautiful heart is important to the Lord. He sees each area of your soul that has felt broken and divided. Today, healing grace is flowing into your life. Where you have experienced trauma, suffered from disappointment, or struggled with fear, the oil of God's love is being poured out. This is your moment to receive.

The Lord is inviting you into supernatural, miraculous freedom. He sees you, beloved. He has heard your cry and He is answering with the power of transformational truth. As you receive these truths in the depths of your being, not just in your mind, you are coming into internal alignment. There is a reset happening—a divine recalibration of your heart. You are moving into a deep place of encounter and communion, where revelation awakens your sleeping faith.

Let the eyes of your heart open now. Come and see Him face to face so fear will have no power over you. In this place of holy communion where you experience the reality of the great I Am living within you, healing manifests.

It's time for truth to explode inside of you! You are a carrier of glory, a partaker of the divine nature, a vessel of His Spirit, and the door between heaven and earth. Lean your head upon His chest and listen. He adores you. He loves you. All He wants is for you to believe.

My Heart's Response

Jesus, above all else, I desire to see You face to face and experience the transforming power of Your love. I step through the doorway of faith that leads me into the arms of Your wraparound Presence and the manifestation of Your promises. What a joy it is to know that You hear me, that You love me. I know I will never be the same as the power of Your truth touches my heart, awakening my sleeping faith.

Thank You for sweeping away the ashes of suffering and creating something beautiful. I can feel Your supernatural faith igniting within my heart and fear losing its grip. Temporary distractions no longer entice me. My gaze is fixed on You. You are my healer.

How blessed I am! You are bringing me into divine alignment with the truths of heaven. I know that every area of my life is being bathed in the oil of Your Presence and revolutionized by Your love, and I will carry this healing balm to others.

Day 2

Shine!

Look at you now—
arising as the dayspring of the dawn,
fair as the shining moon,
bright and brilliant as the sun in all its strength—
astonishing to behold as a majestic army
waving banners of victory.
Song of Songs 6:10 TPT

In every realm of existence, the Creator has all authority. He holds the keys to unlock the unseen realm. He is God, the King of the Universe, the supreme and majestic One, who lives inside of you. All of heaven is waiting in anticipation for you to walk in the Kingdom power and authority that has been granted to you. From before the beginning of time, the Father saw this moment with you in it.

He's calling you to awaken to the truth of who you are in Christ. Nothing can overpower Jesus' bride when she understands her identity. Look at Him, beloved. The more you do, the more you will understand the gravity of your importance on the earth.

The manifestation of God's glory through you is His dream. You are a shining one! The treasure chest of unfolding revelation is open to you. Come, receive truths that will blast you into a different way of living—

an ascended lifestyle where you see your glorious King in every situation. As you follow His lead and reflect His nature, you will shine into the darkness and set the captives free. The great unveiling of Christ in you will release people into freedom. Today, agree with who God says you are.

My Heart's Response

Jesus, everything changes when we stand face to face. As I look into Your eyes, faith reignites within me and lies lose their grip on my soul. The power of Jesus' costly love releases me from fear and causes me to sing. I am who You say I am: loved, chosen, a perfect partner for You. I am Your shining one, as fair as the moon, as bright and brilliant as the sun.

Thank You for inviting me to taste the power of the age to come, for clothing me in Your righteousness and filling me with Your glory. As I keep my heart tuned into heaven, I will hear Your voice and follow Your lead. Fill me to overflowing so Your glory radiates through my face and drips from every word. Together, we will walk hand in hand and I will declare Your love to the world around me.

Day 3

The Interior Life

Set your mind on things above, not on things on the earth.
For you died, and your life is hidden with Christ in God.
Colossians 3:2-3 NKJV

Jesus wants to reset us back to the vibrant, abundant, interior reality of life in the Spirit. Our union with Christ is what enables encounters with Him. The issue is sensitization. Our spirits, not our souls, were designed to lead in subjection to His Spirit. This means a realignment and internal shifting of our attention. As we learn to refocus our conscious awareness on our oneness with Jesus, our souls begin to relinquish control, and our spirits are strengthened.

The life of the Spirit is experienced and maintained in the interior life. It is cultivated by practicing His Presence in every situation and turning our gaze to our spirit and Christ within. By doing this, we mentally let go of everything in our external world that our soul is interacting with. We simply relinquish control, remind our soul to live in its highest state, and shift from a natural experience to a supernatural one.

When our spirit leads, the strength of Christ becomes ours, and our soul is released from the oppressive burden of carrying the weight of life. The highest choice we can make is to gaze at Christ, who is now within us. When we gently say to our soul, “Perform your highest created task; look at Jesus within,” healing cascades through the doorway of our spirit, bathing our emotions and central nervous system. If distracting emotions and thoughts pop up, we can stay locked onto Jesus. He is a magnet; He is the stronger solution and He draws us to Himself.

My Heart’s Response

Lord, You are the most amazing teacher. Thank You for instructing me in the ways of grace and showing me that life in the Spirit is as easy as shifting my gaze to You. Right now, my soul lets go of the false responsibility to fix everything and breathes a sigh of relief. Your soothing, supernatural love is healing every chamber of my soul. I am stepping into the deeper spiritual life, where I choose to practice Your Presence in every situation and allow my soul to rest.

My heart is soaring with joy at this new reality. This is Your gift to me and I receive it wholeheartedly. My heart is fixed on You, positioned in absolute trust and rest. Over and over again, I will choose You. I will look at You and allow my spirit to follow Your lead.

Day 4

Nothing Will Separate Us

Listen! I hear my lover's voice.
I know it's him coming to me—
leaping with joy over mountains,
skipping in love over the hills that separate us,
to come to me.
Song of Songs 2:8 TPT

Jesus wants to remove the landing places of the enemy in our hearts. These are the areas with unhealed trauma or where we find ourselves going into fear-driven self-preservation. Today, as you bask in the Lord's Presence, notice painful memories or trauma that come to the surface, and receive His healing love at the very root of that pain. Your soul may feel battered, but God's Word transforms. You are changed by every unfolding revelation that you embrace.

This Song of Songs experience is for you. Let it become real to you. Say *yes* to Jesus as He skips over the hills that have caused you to feel separate from Him. He is healing you. He is gazing into your soul, even into the darkest areas, and pouring out His love. The Light of the world is shining into your heart and kissing you awake.

As you relax into the arms of grace, the landing places of this fear-driven self-preservation are completely demolished. The enemy has been disarmed. You are experiencing the finished work of the Cross. The power of Jesus' blood has removed the power of the enemy in your life! Freedom belongs to you.

My Heart's Response

I'm Yours, Jesus. I am Yours. My thought life, my mind, and my emotions do not belong to the enemy, they belong to You. Every aspect of my life—past, present, and future, is Yours. You said the enemy had no claim on you, and I echo that declaration. Your Presence lives in me; therefore, I too declare that satan has no claim on me.

It is no longer I who lives, but it is You, Jesus, who lives in me. This is Your body. The enemy cannot have possession of this body which is the temple of the Holy Spirit of Yahweh, of the Living God, forever and on into eternity.

The same Spirit that raised You from the dead is pulsating through my body, soul, and spirit right now. I'm so grateful that I am not a victim of a defeated demon! I am royalty on the earth, manifesting the majesty of God. You are the source, Jesus, and I am the expression of You in oneness. Thank You that nothing separates me from You.

Day 5

The Sound of Freedom

A Prophetic Word

Arise, my love, my beautiful companion,
and run with me to the higher place.
For now is the time to arise and come away with me.
Song of Songs 2:13 TPT

I am awakening My sleeping ones, awakening the places where you have been lulled into powerlessness, where you have been dulled and depressed. I am bringing forth the sound of My life in you. Where you have felt spiritually hard of hearing, now you will hear Me. Lean in and listen by faith. I am delivering you from oppression and despair. The frequency of heaven is vibrating inside of you. Loneliness, isolation, and rejection are literally being shaken off of you. I am setting you free.

You are being released as a pure sound within the Creator's grand symphony. Today you will grow in awareness. You will experience more completely your redeemed oneness with Me. This is your sound: My life in you. This is your new nature: Christ in you, the hope of glory. The sound of who I am is rising inside of you. Do you feel it? From the depths of holy union, a roar, the sound of My strength and passion, shattering the obstacles in your life.

Sing with Me, beloved. Roar with Me! Rejoice, for I am bringing you forth right now! Your barren season has ended. Will you agree with Me? Will you stop rehearsing the negative and fix your gaze on Me? I gave everything to prove My love to you. Take My hand and let us run together into the sound of freedom.

My Heart's Response

Yes, I agree, Jesus! My barren season has ended. Thank You for strengthening me and reminding me that our union isn't affected by my circumstances. I am never alone. Nothing will separate me from Your love. The sound of new life is rising within me, spilling over and washing away the debris of oppression.

I feel Your passion roaring inside of me, igniting my faith. I cast off the heavy garments of doubt and fear. They do not belong to me. I am clothed in glory and I am awakening to who I am in You. I am powerful. I am the joy of Your heart and with Your hand wrapped securely around mine, You are calling me to run with You. I am not afraid of what lies ahead, for You are with me.

Day 6

The Strength of Union

But the one who is united and joined to the Lord is one spirit with Him.
1 Corinthians 6:17 AMP

As children of the Most High God, separation from Him is a deception. We are not separate; we are one. The grace of the Gospel of Jesus Christ is that we live out of His strength in this union reality. The more we tune into our oneness with Him and live from there, the more we experience Him in every circumstance.

Abandon and trust accelerate us into this way of living. Instead of trying to live in our own strength, we consistently turn our gaze to Christ within and recall this holy union. We sit back in Him and surrender our will and our way for His. As we yield control and refuse to make decisions about our impossible situation without Him, He moves to fix it instead of us.

The more we choose to live with our spirit leading, the more quickly we will notice if our soul attempts to take over. In every instance, we can turn into the Christ within and ask Him how He views our situation. We can ask, "Who do you want to be for me or through me in this situation, Jesus?" In this way, our hearts more consistently live in the experience of His love, with His life dispensing through us. By practicing our oneness with Him, it becomes natural and we effortlessly flow in the strength of oneness within.

My Heart's Response

Yes, Lord! This is exactly what I desire—to live continually aware of our unbreakable, impenetrable union. From now on, I will choose to remain mindful of our oneness, so no attempt to devour my relationship with You can succeed. I am not weak. I do not stand alone like prey for the enemy. This is Your promise to me—I am strong because we are one! Thank You for this glorious deliverance from the lies of the enemy.

I dive into the ocean of Your love, eternally immersed, captivated by You. And by looking at You, Jesus, I see life through Your eyes. You are the strength of my heart and my portion forever. Your life is flowing through every cell of my body. Nothing can separate me from You! No weapon formed against me can prosper. In every decision, trial, and test, You strengthen me and lead me by Your Spirit. Our union has breathed faith into my heart again.

Day 7

Experiencing Heaven's Reality

There's a private place reserved for the devoted lovers of Yahweh,
where they sit near him and receive
the revelation-secrets of his promises.
Psalm 25:14 TPT

Today, the Lord is releasing His perfect wisdom to you. He's inviting you to go higher, into a perception shift that lifts you out of earthly-mindedness into heavenly-mindedness. This is your moment of 'glory to glory' transformation. He is pouring out grace to surrender all so that you can know Him as your everything.

As you release your cares and set aside distractions, He draws you into an unquestionable experience of Christ within. Through this revelation of who He is inside of you, you're released into perfect peace, the expectation of victory, and the strength of His majesty in every situation.

Lean into this Perfect One and discover His sovereignty and unmatched love. This is His desire for you—that His truth and His Word become experiential as He infuses, imprints, and expands Himself into you. Because of this, He is no longer only something you know about, but He is experienced with unquestionable certainty.

As you practice living in this new reality, He demolishes mindsets that are contrary to Him. You will begin to see Jesus meeting every need and sharing the deeper things of His life. You will interface with the world while resting internally in His arms. As His Presence becomes your habit, you consequently find everything you need.

My Heart's Response

Jesus, this is my desire—to know You, to experience the reality of You inside of me in a way that leaves no room for doubt. And because I know this is Your desire as well, I reach with a faith-soaked heart to receive a fresh revelation. Thank You that You have come to infuse all that You are into this vessel of flesh. You are changing my internal world and sensitizing me to Your holy and most beautiful Spirit. You are becoming more real than the world around me.

I choose You over everything else that vies for my attention, drawing from heaven's reality so it will frame my own. As I sink into the bliss of our oneness, I will see You in every aspect, showing up with direction, wisdom, and favor. Every mindset that has restricted me is coming into alignment with the truth of who You are. Everything about my life is changing now because You are showcasing Your majesty in me.

Day 8

The Appearing

And he who loves Me will be loved by My Father,
and I will love him and manifest Myself to him.
John 14:21 NKJV

This scripture in the original language means, *I will fully reveal Myself to him and personally appear to him.* The Lord wants to encounter those who love Him. Imagine that! Isn't that glorious? It's in the Word! Your desire to see Him and know Him is a desire planted in you by God.

Today, Jesus is smashing everything off of you that has been warring against this being your every-moment reality. It doesn't mean you'll walk in a full-blown encounter every minute of the day, but sensing Him, seeing and smelling Him, feeling Him, your heart being exhilarated by the truth. These are all facets of encounter and life with Jesus.

Your heart's little movements toward Him in love are powerful! As you choose to love Him, you continuously rise from glory to glory. In this posture of love, you stand in victory above anything that comes against your life; stately and secure, as you share with Jesus your heart. As you share with Him your vineyard of love, literally giving Him your love, this desire to be with Him grows and grows and grows. The

Word promises that as you do you that, Jesus will personally appear to you. These are not my words; they're His. They are His precious and personal promise to you.

My Heart's Response

Jesus, I'm overwhelmed by the promise of seeing and encountering You! What we've shared up to this point has been wonderful and amazing, but I long for more of You. Nothing matters more to me than knowing You. To live in this moment-by-moment reality, where Your nearness is my consistent awareness, is my heart's desire.

I'm so grateful that You don't hide from me but tenderly draw me close, so I can commune with You face to face. Your grace has created a pathway for me to walk on, and it leads straight to You. I will not strive in my pursuit. I will simply take Your hand and walk step by step with You. My eyes are on You, Lord. My heart is fixed on the Lover of my soul. Whether You manifest in Your quiet home inside me or appear in glory before me, You are my every-moment reality.

Day 9

Until Lambs Become Lions

They will walk after the Lord [in obedience and worship],
Who will roar like a lion;
He will roar [summoning them]...
Hosea 11:10 AMP

In a vision, I saw Queen Elizabeth wearing a beige garment, symbolizing humility. Over it was a fine covering of chainmail, signifying protection. She was dragging a huge sword made of oak, which speaks of the Word of God coming out of us as oaks of righteousness (see Is 61:3). On the side of the sword were the words, "Rise and rise again, until lambs become lions." It wasn't until I researched that I learned it was a quote from the movie Robin Hood.

This is what the Father is doing; He's moving us from being lambs to becoming lions. We will always be precious lambs wrapped around our Shepherd's neck and carefully held. But there is a magnificent transfiguration occurring within us. It is the expression of Jesus as the Lion of the tribe of Judah, the King, and the Word, all manifesting in us in great power. He is teaching us of our unquestionable authority.

We are lovers of Jesus, operating from oneness and intimacy with Him, completely secure in His love. It is from this place of resting and trusting in His sovereignty that we radiate with majestic power and rise in our identity. Regardless of what we face, we rise and rise again. We brush off every lie that we 'cannot' or 'are not', and choose to remember who we are. We are His! We are complete in Christ and we are roaring our agreement today!

My Heart's Response

Jesus, my heart is saturated in Your love and I am rising in confidence, secure in Your love. You are my conquering King who has defeated every foe. I'm undone, overwhelmed with gratefulness because You are with me, in me, and roaring through me. You are teaching me to stand in the authority I have through You.

This is my heart's desire—to never be out of step with You. Whether You ask me to pour out compassion or demolish the enemy's plan, I will remain in sync with You, doing what we see the Father do. I am living from the secret place, the epicenter of all power and dominion. As I commune with You here, power is being released from my life.

Day 10

I Am Transforming You

A Prophetic Word

For he enjoys his faithful lovers.
He adorns the humble with his beauty,
and he loves to give them victory.
Psalm 149:4 TPT

You are Mine, and I am yours. You are My greatest treasure. I am fashioning you and forming you into My glorious bride. I'm melting away the things that have damaged you. I am your healer who enfolds you with the strength of who I am. I will do wonders in your life.

I see you. I see into the depths of your soul. Look into My eyes. All that I am, I give to you. All that I have, I share with you. My covenant with you is unbreakable. You are safe with Me. I'm alive in the very center of your being and we are one: you in Me and I in you. I am that I am. I am all that you will ever need. I am the light inside of you, the glory radiating out of you.

Before the foundation of the world, I chose you. You are royalty. There will be a great unveiling of who I am in you and through you. But first, let Me consume you with the majestic wonder of who I am so you may walk in wholeness. Then, as you live out the wonder of our union, reflecting the beauty of My love into the world, hearts will be revived. Simply open yourself to Me today without hesitation or reservation, and taste the fullness of who I am within you.

My Heart's Response

Jesus, I feel the breath of heaven upon my soul. The dusty remains of lowly thinking are being blown away by Your glory wind. You are transforming me and making me whole. Thank You for encouraging me, for knowing me so completely, for choosing me, and calling me to run with You. As I lock eyes with You, the truth of Who You are adjusts the lens of my perception and I can see clearly. Hope, unbridled joy, and faith are bubbling inside of me. I can breathe again!

I am Your bride, whose beauty emanates from our love connection. You have clothed me in a splendor more glorious than the angels. Unveil Yourself within me and radiate out. I have no desire to draw others to myself but only to bring You glory so that others may know Your love.

Day 11

The Pillar of Fire Within

He who overcomes (is victorious),
I will make him a pillar in the sanctuary of My God...
Revelation 3:12 AMPC

We are immovable pillars in the temple of our God. We are solid, becoming secure in our identity as we prioritize heart-to-heart connection with Him. Jesus has filled us with His nature and divine strength. His fiery passion burns deep within, and we have been commissioned to release it into the world. As we become everything that He is—love, wisdom, mercy, might, etc., we can uphold and support His Kingdom's purposes.

The One who is a Pillar of Fire is within you. You contain the unshakable, unyielding seat of power and authority. Your heart has become the Holy of Holies. That is why the enemy goes after your heart—it's where God, and your source of power, reside.

The One who is perfect, governmental authority longs for you to take your stand with Him. As you become certain of your solidity in Christ, you will live as a victorious overcomer. God has given you the grace and strength to experience victory continuously. No matter what you go through, as you draw from His divine life inside you, you will rise from one degree of glory to the next. You will stand as an immovable pillar, watching His testimony increase in the earth through you. There's nothing the enemy can bring against your life that God will not work together for your good because you are called according to His purposes.

My Heart's Response

Jesus, You are the source of power within me, the Pillar of Fire who burns away the lies that I have believed. As I tune in to You, Your Presence stabilizes me, faith begins flooding me, and Your victory becomes established in my heart. Thank You for making Your home in me and for sealing these truths in my spirit. All that You are, You are inside of me.

The fire of Your glory is consuming every mindset that has contradicted the truth of my identity. I am rising now, standing in the authority You have entrusted to me. I am Your awakening, radiant, victorious, and overcoming bride. Glorify Yourself through me so that my life may bring You honor and others may know Your love. You are the victory that has overcome every obstacle in my life! I am complete in Christ.

Day 12

Living in the Flow

My old identity has been co-crucified with Christ and no longer lives. And now the essence of this new life is no longer mine, for the Anointed One lives his life through me—we live in union as one! My new life is empowered by the faith of the Son of God who loves me so much that he gave himself for me, dispensing his life into mine!
Galatians 2:20 TPT

Our spiritual wealth is in God, like hidden treasure waiting to be discovered—heaven's wisdom and endless riches of revelation knowledge. Just as you received Jesus our Messiah by faith, so you continue your journey of faith, progressing further into this holy union. Having a heart that looks to God and is devoted to Him is the key. This is what causes your spiritual roots to go deep in Him. This is the doorway to go deeper.

The Lord has enabled us to live from a place of utter saturation and immersion in His Presence. He is tuning our senses to the continuous flow of the river of His Presence, so we can abide there. We can live from the awareness of His nature within us instead of in the buffeting of horizontal relationships, reactions, and controlling self-preservation.

Jesus is a ferocious force of love that dissolves every harm aimed against us. As we live connected to His expressions of love, all negativity or behaviors that come at us get absorbed into the light of His Presence. When this constant awareness of Him becomes our normal, our responses will be seen in explosions of healing and transformational love. Our flow of union with Him will continue uninterrupted; fully present, fully engaged, pouring into the world around us.

My Heart's Response

Lord, I want nothing to inhibit the flow of Your Spirit working in and through me. Thank You that I can live as You did, doing nothing other than what You saw our Father doing. Absorb me into Your glorious light until I am no longer recognizable. When people look at me, I want them to see You, to hear You, and to experience the tangible touch of Your eternal love.

Take my heart, life, every dream, and each moment of my attention and weave Yourself into each one. I want nothing more than to walk in this life-altering revelation of our oneness. You have poured yourself into me, so saturate me entirely, and together we will quench the thirst of others.

Day 13

Entwined With Him

But those who wait on the Lord
Shall renew their strength;
They shall mount up with wings like eagles,
They shall run and not be weary,
They shall walk and not faint.
Isaiah 40:31 NKJV

This verse would be better translated, "They that entwine with the Lord's thoughts will renew their strength." Though many Bible versions use the word 'wait', the Hebrew word is 'qâvâh' (kaw-vaw) which, correctly translated, means 'to entwine'. The Strong's definition says, in part, 'to bind together (perhaps by twisting)'. This is the grace that the Lord is releasing—as we entwine with His thoughts, we are strengthened.

If you want to renew your strength, rise and fly, run spiritually, physically, and emotionally strong, be filled with abundant, vibrant life, this is how you do it—entwine with the Lord's thoughts. Become obsessed with Him, where everything that He is, the great I AM, is all you see, all that you think about, all you live for. He becomes the substance of every desire. You see Him in every moment and each situation.

When you look into His eyes, you see your reflection, and everything changes—you increasingly discover that all that He is, you are. You are His mirror image. His nature is your nature. His wisdom is your wisdom. All that He is. Not part of Him, but all that Jesus is, is who you are in this world. Continue entwining with Him, and you will be an unstoppable force.

My Heart's Response

Lord, I say *yes* to this invitation to entwine with You. This is what I long for—to know You and to experience our oneness. To stand inside of You as You stand inside of me so that my every thought flows in harmony with Yours. I want to see through Your eyes and love with perfect, untainted love. I want to soar on the wind of Your breath, as the eagles do—above every obstacle. Thank You that as I live from this place of prioritizing You, every part of my being is transformed.

Jesus, I will love You and live for You in the manner in which You deserve. I will entwine with You so that all I am is consumed, overtaken by this reality of holy union. I sense Your extravagant love pouring into me, filling my being with the fullness of who You are. I want nothing more than to live each second entwined with You, aware of You in the core of my being.

Day 14

Heaven to Earth

Your kingdom come.
Your will be done
On earth as it is in heaven.
Matthew 6:10 NKJV

When Jesus told us to pray "…on earth as it is in heaven", He was encouraging us to see what's happening there so we can bring it to earth. He wants us to believe that living from heaven to earth is our birthright as children of God. Jesus' blood enables us to do this. As we know and engage Him, not just in periodic encounters, but as a constant reality, we will live in our authority. When we sit in the One who is perfect government and do what we see Him doing, we will live governmentally.

We've been those who carry a form of godliness yet lack power. We've peered through a glass dimly when we've been called to see Him face to face. Jesus calls us to live in the Spirit, rise out of our natural timeline and see reality from His perspective. When we do this and engage with it, we can live from there.

He has called us to be perfect as He is, so it's critical that we constantly engage with the One who is perfect. We must lean into the One who is the fullness of wisdom. We have been invited to live aware of the all-powerful One inside us so that we can manifest Him in the earth. This is our inheritance. This is our honor.

My Heart's Response

Jesus, I see You standing inside of me, powerful and wise, dripping with love. All that You are, You are in me. I want nothing in my life, thoughts, or belief systems to hinder Your flow through me. I want to live so connected to this heavenly reality, that my eyes continually behold You and constantly see what You're doing. To forever remain in tune with Your Spirit, as I live each day as Your representative on this earth.

Thank You for the grace that enables me to let natural distractions fade away. Though the busyness of life sometimes muffles the sound of grace, I'm so grateful that with one movement of my heart, I can tune back in. I am captured by Your amazing love all over again. And in this place, I stand in my authority, wrapped with You, knowing who I am and who I represent. We are an unrelenting source of love on the earth.

Day 15

All That I Am

A Prophetic Word

And God said to Moses, "I AM WHO I AM."
Exodus 3:14 NKJV

Transfix your gaze on Me. Become consumed, obsessed with the Person of I Am. I live and move and have My being in you. You live and move and have your being in Me. I am your life. All that I am is who you are. All that I am is the very substance of your being. I have already given you all of Me. All that I am is alive inside of you. I am closer than your breath.

You have all of Me, beloved. There is no part of My goodness, love, or power that has been held back from you. Simply receive what you have need of. Let the fullness of My divinity overtake you. Rest in the reality of who I am for you. I am everything that you could possibly need. I've given you the grace to gaze, to see who I am with fresh eyes. See Me pouring Myself into every situation that has left you weary.

I have given you everything you need that pertains to life and godliness. I am your provision, wisdom, hope, and your abundant supply. I am peace, comfort, and love. I am the answer to every question you've ever asked. Inside of Me, where you live and move and have your being, is the greatness of all that I am, and I am calling you forth.

My Heart's Response

Jesus, I want to stay right here, in the reality of Your magnificent love, forever. You are enlightening my eyes to see and my heart to fully receive the reality of I Am inside of me. You have made me one with You, so regardless of what I face, I can remain tuned in to You. Thank You that I can sit back into Your headship and gaze.

Every incorrect, natural perspective that has framed my life and my 'normal' that has created confusion or fear, I exchange it now for Your eternal truth. You are everything I need and all that I desire. You truly are my magnificent and holy obsession. I surrender my life to You and hold nothing back. I have no desire to run my own life, Jesus. You are the truth that has changed me. It is no longer I who live because the fullness of who You are has taken over.

Day 16

Love That Transforms

Let us arise and run to the vineyards of your people
and see if the budding vines of love are now in full bloom.
We will discover if their passion is awakened.
There I will display my love for you.
Song of Songs 7:12 TPT

Jesus is opening the deepest parts of Himself to you because He wants you to know Him. His kiss is awakening the parts of your heart that have been asleep, and now the revelation of Jesus being your Bridegroom King will become reality.

This most-precious One has extended His hand, inviting you into a divine dance of transformational love. If you accept this offer, if you will step right up to Him and take His hand, He will draw you closer than you've ever experienced before. The foundation of your life is being laid in place—it is the foundation of love.

Knowing Him isn't head knowledge. It is a living experience becoming tangible to our hearts. He is tuning us into who He is on an entirely different level, where the fullness of His Presence in us becomes a reality. As we live from this place, it transforms us. It enables us to flow with Him without restriction, and when we do, everything in the created realm responds to the Creator in us.

The more intimately we know Him, the more power drips from our lives. Effortlessly, we stand in Him on this earth as living portals, living invitations, enabling others to remember who they truly are.

My Heart's Response

Jesus, this is what I want—to know You more than I ever have before. To experience the wonder of Your glory in every cell, and know beyond a shadow of a doubt that all that You are is coursing through my veins. I want to feel it. To be absolutely wrecked by Your perfect love so that I am never the same, always looking and sounding more like You. Flood me with this reality until every part of me responds and my soul is consumed by Your Spirit.

Thank You for drawing me with cords of love and purifying me. Thank You for establishing these incredible truths deep within me. This is how I will live now—eyes fixed on Yours, as You teach and lead me. I will live in the intoxication of our holy union until all of me is eternally entwined with Your love. Moving as one, we welcome others into our divine dance.

Day 17

Stand in His Victory

I have told you these things, so that in Me you may have [perfect] peace. ...be courageous [be confident, be undaunted, be filled with joy]; I have overcome the world." [My conquest is accomplished, My victory abiding.]

John 16:33 AMP

Many have been inhibited by the crushing traumas of life, but Jesus is liberating us. He is overturning the war that has desensitized us from experiencing the bliss of Christ. The past will no longer define us. Everything that has sat in the gates of our souls, hindering our awareness of His Presence, is being exposed and cleansed by the power of His blood. It is time to experience the finished work of the Cross.

The Light of the world is shining in our hearts, and when He shines, the enemy retreats. We have been redeemed by the Redeemer and Restorer of all things. Right now, Jesus is ready to thoroughly saturate us in His love, until no chamber of our heart is left dry.

As we accept His offer and stay close to Him, fear dissipates. We may still feel fear, but it will no longer counsel or influence our hearts. We are shifting from being victims of our circumstances into overcomers, strengthened by our Redeemer. As we surrender to Him and practice living from the secret place of His Presence, Jesus will showcase His majesty in our lives. As our internal world changes, so our external reality changes. We will increasingly experience a state of inner rest, peace, and expectation of victory.

My Heart's Response

Jesus, I surrender. I've tried so hard to fix things in my own strength and failed miserably. But I'm done. I take my hands off and surrender afresh to You. I'm getting out of the way so that You can take over. Thank You for the cleansing power of Your blood that washes my thinking and aligns it perfectly with Yours. From this place, I know I can think clearly. I can breathe again. Fear has lost this battle. The Blood has roared its mighty voice.

Your perfect wisdom counsels me now. I feel the effects of darkness sliding off, as lies bow to Your glorious light within me. You are my strength. Your arms are my safe place, my secret hideaway. This is where I will live, forever. From this place, everything around me looks different. My past doesn't intimidate me any longer and I'm not afraid of the future. You are the only thing that defines my life. You are with me, and nothing can separate me from Your love.

Day 18

Breathe Him In

At the very moment I called out to you, you answered me!
You strengthened me deep within my soul and breathed fresh courage into me.
Psalm 138:3 TPT

This is your moment to experience the Lord, your moment for encounter and transformation. Whatever you need, the One who is the solution is right here, within you. He's closer than your breath! He surrounds and enfolds you completely. You may have been troubled, busy, and distracted, but as you tune back into the reality of His Presence, every pressure will melt away. Set your thoughts and the affections of your heart on Jesus right now.

Take this time which you have set aside, to breathe in the life-giving substance of His love, and breathe out the pressures of life. See the Lord escorting you into the miracle of this moment. Take slow, deep breaths as you become conscious again of His Spirit within you. Breathe Him in, and as you exhale, release each care.

Angels are ministering to you. Focus your attention on the Lord and center your internal world, the attention of your heart, onto the truth of Christ in you. The glory of God, the amazing treasure of His being, fully and absolutely resides inside of you. As you resign yourself entirely to the Lord, He is absorbing you into His Presence. He is re-sensitizing you to His whisper. In the quiet of this moment, notice the peace that is being released to you. Stay in this place and rest here until all else fades away, but Him!

My Heart's Response

Jesus, You are so holy. You always know exactly what I need. Thank You for the cascading peace that is pouring into me right now. My desire is to remain centered in the awareness of Your magnificent life inside of me. Holy Spirit, flood my entire being with fresh light. Shine into every dark shadow and every lie. Illuminate the blockages that hinder my ability to experience Your glory. I want nothing to muddy the waters of my heart.

As I breathe You in, re-sensitize me to Your voice. You've already torn the veil that would dim my vision, so I look by faith with eyes that see. I look to You and nothing else. I tune everything else out so that I may see the Beautiful One. Jesus, thank You for this next level, this new and abundant measure of grace that You are dispensing into my soul.

Day 19

His Glory Through You

For all who belong to me now belong to you.
And all who belong to you now belong to me as well,
and my glory is revealed through their surrendered lives
John 17:10 TPT

Divine and natural, dust and deity—we are entwined with Christ and have become one being. We are His perfect ones, a new creation filled with divinity. As we align with this extraordinary truth, awakening and acceleration happen inside of us. Jesus longs for us to live from the revelation of this truth: the uncontaminated purity of Christ dwells in us.

When we live completely and continually in this reality, knowing who we are, our eyes become clear. We see our calling to co-reign with Jesus for the restoration of all things. It is our destiny to govern in the nature and authority of I AM.

Jesus said you would do greater works than He did. You have been activated to touch broken humanity with compassion and power, to heal the sick, see minds restored and hearts set free. Signs, wonders, and miracles will flow through your hands as you reach out to others. It is your birthright to experience an even greater manifestation of the Kingdom of heaven than what occurred in Jesus' life.

Faith makes the switch. Faith connects you to the miraculous. If you don't see these things happening as you step out, don't quit! You are who He says you are. You are His perfect one, filled with the fullness of Christ, and called to pour His glory into the earth. Continue to follow His lead, and you will experience supernatural power flooding through you into every situation.

My Heart's Response

Jesus, my heart comes into agreement with Yours. I believe I am filled with Your supreme power and authority. Divine nature is now my nature. The power of God, to which everything must yield, is present within me. Thank You for flooding the eyes of my understanding with the strength of this revelation. I want to run with You in unprecedented levels of glory and see Your desires come to pass.

This mystery of God embedded within me is igniting my faith. As I meditate on the wonder of this truth, I feel Your heart for others. Show me how to share this heavenly treasure chest of hope. I want to partner with You to pour out the riches of Your glory and awaken the sleeping hearts around me. Make Your passion my passion. Flow through my willing heart.

Day 20

Lord of Every Situation

Now, the "Lord" I'm referring to is the Holy Spirit, and wherever he is Lord, there is freedom.

2 Corinthians 3:17 TPT

Jesus wants a relationship with us where we trust Him with absolutely everything. As you read today's entry, if you realize you're holding onto anything that He's asked for, release it to Him. Let's relinquish control and bring everything back under His headship. We can trust the Lord with the most precious people and situations of our lives. Nothing we give Him can be snatched from His hands. It is all safe with Him. As we release control and let every care flow to Him, Jesus steps in with fresh, divine intervention.

Our Beloved wants to delight your heart by the way He moves on your behalf. He wants to thrill you with answers and breakthroughs that only He can bring. It's time to stop trying to figure it all out. Let Jesus be Lord over every single concern. He wants to wow you, to make you feel loved and captivated by the divine romance of your relationship. He wants to show you His faithfulness.

This is the steady walk—where we are so obsessed with Him that we cannot be distracted by trials. When our hearts are absolutely convinced and utterly gripped by the undeniable reality of His trustworthy love, we stand stable and immovable. Everything in our life becomes saturated with light, and we see His goodness overflowing in every situation. Jesus is giving us the capacity to truly believe with every fiber of our being, with zero unbelief and zero concern. Nothing compares to the magnificence, perfection, beauty, and love of who He is.

My Heart's Response

Jesus, I bring every area of my heart under Your Lordship and trust You with my life. I only want to sit under Your influence, where I am not moved by anything that comes against me. You are my protector, wisdom, and abundant source for every need. I take my hands off of every situation that I'm facing in my life, mind, body, relationships, or finances, and trust that they are safely held in Yours.

Holy Spirit, I declare that You are Lord, and where You are Lord, there is freedom. I give You absolute power over my life and ask You to reign as the one magnificent influence in my life. Jesus, with fresh dedication, I submit to You as Lord. I believe You are moving in and through my life at a different level.

Day 21

Your Devoted Heart

A Prophetic Word

May your tender love overwhelm me, O Lord,
for you are my Savior and you keep your promises.
Psalm 119:41 TPT

Beautiful one, the expressions of your heart mean so much to Me. I have heard your cries of longing in the secret place. I know your desire to go deeper with Me, be healed, have heavenly encounters, and know Me more. You have dared to believe and step toward Me. You have bravely opened your tender heart again for My holy kiss, daring to believe the kiss is for you. You have accepted My invitation into this divine romance, and now I am gently touching the fragile places and wrapping them in My healing love.

Your devoted heart has touched Me deeply. I honor your courage in daring to trust that I will love and meet you in both your places of pain and your places of desire. I am gently unfolding your tightly protective arms from across your chest, and I'm breathing my Spirit-kiss into your heart.

Close your eyes and feel My holy breath blowing into the areas that have been locked, self-preserved, and where you have not been able to let go and trust fully. The power of My love is freeing you now. Those chains that once bound and restricted your faith are lying at your feet! You are standing in Me now. You are established in Me. We are one. Enter into the joy of absolute abandon and radical trust. You are free!

My Heart's Response

Jesus, I let go and surrender every lie, every bit of filth that I have believed that is not in agreement with Your heart for me. I give it to You now. I relinquish control, Jesus. I surrender my reputation, my past, my money, and every idol that has falsely fed my heart's security. Thank You for Your miracle-working, life-transforming, all-powerful, all-consuming, perfect life, which is completely engulfing me and radiating out of me.

Your light is bursting into every corner of my heart! I take every inch of my being back from the clutches of darkness right now and I give myself afresh to You. I trust You to free me now in ways I have longed for. Your liquid light is rejuvenating me in the depths of my soul and body. Thank You, Jesus, for this divine transformation!

Day 22

The King of Glory Within

Now you are ready, my bride,
to come with me as we climb the highest peaks together.
Come with me through the archway of trust.
Song of Songs 4:8 TPT

I saw an archway open in the spirit, which Jesus called the Archway of Faith. He stood on the other side of the arch, as the majestic King of Glory, beckoning me to come to Him. Power radiated from His being. His love drew me and exhilarated me. It was holy and tangible. The purity of who He is poured into me. As I stepped into the arch, I went into Him. I merged into Jesus as the King, and we became one.

Thousands of angels surrounded us as Jesus showed off His bride. See yourself as I saw us—the bride clothed in a golden robe, holding a scepter, wearing a crown, and shining with His nature. The angels marvel at the royalty and expression of His Kingship inside of us.

This is heaven's perspective and the revelation He is breathing into us today—the wonder of Jesus, the King of Glory, within us. If we open our hearts to this, it will ignite the awe of God in great humility. The spirit of the fear of the Lord will transform our character. We will be empowered to walk in a greater degree of holiness, compassion, and power when we set ourselves apart for Him without compromise.

Confident in Him, we will release redemptive power as He leads us each day.

My Heart's Response

Jesus, I see myself in a new way, and I am awed by the holiness of this truth—I am filled with the King of Glory. Thank You for inviting me to run with You in ministry. Yes, I will run with You! This is my desire—to look like love, leaning, as a mature bride and expression of holiness. Purify me, Your bride, so I will shine with the glory You have entrusted me with. Let there be no remaining sensation of separation—one heart and mind with You.

Make Your desire my own so that I carry the authority of heaven in purity. May my mouth drip with the wisdom of Your love, releasing words of truth. My heart echoes the Shulamite's, "I've made up my mind, until the darkness disappears and the dawn has fully come, in spite of shadows and fears, I will go to the mountaintop with You, Jesus, the mountaintop of suffering love and the hill of burning incense. Yes, I will be Your bride (see SOS 4:6)."

Day 23

Breaking off False Identity

Now, if all were included in his death, they were equally included in his resurrection. This unveiling of his love redefines human life. Whatever reference we could have of ourselves outside of our association with Christ is no longer relevant.

2 Corinthians 5:15-16 TMSB

Everything outside of Christ's definition of who we are as a new creation, as His image, His perfect ones, is irrelevant. Any interpretation we have of ourselves or that has come from others, which doesn't agree with Jesus, is a lie. The only label that carries significance is the one He has given us.

Today, I pray for you, in agreement with Jesus, and break off of your heart any remaining false definitions of who you are. I break the power of every lie and anything that's claimed your identity or contradicts the truth of who you are in Christ. The Father called forth your life and future before the foundation of the earth. You have been called to steward ultimate authority and co-reign with Him. You are the perfect image of the living God!

Receive this freedom in the very core of your being. From the moment of conception until now, any identity that you've accepted which contradicts who you are in Christ is irrelevant. It is irrelevant according to the Word of God. It does not exist anymore. Allow this truth to come alive in you and bring healing and wholeness to your heart. You are His beloved who is rising from one degree of glory to another. You are the Lord's great reward.

My Heart's Response

Lord, all that I am belongs to You. Thank You for pouring the water of the Word into my heart and washing it clean of the lies I was believing. I am who You say I am. I am Your inheritance, the one You died for. Root me and ground me in this truth so that it continues to grow and becomes established in my heart. Let every part of my being absorb the magnitude of this revelation—my surrendered life is Your reward. You love me without reservation.

It is my destiny to know You, to be found in You, living completely saturated with Your glory, to be constantly amazed by the majesty and beauty of my God. This is my heart's desire and true journey. This is the joy of my life! I say *yes* to Your invitation to live in the awe and wonder of who You are, continually, like the Seraphim and Cherubim who surround the throne.

Day 24

Suffering Love

My spirit arose to open for more of his touch. As I surrendered to him, I began to sense his fragrance—the fragrance of his suffering love! It was the sense of myrrh flowing all through me!

Song of Song 5:5 TPT

The place of suffering love offers us something we cannot find anywhere else. This is where we discover Jesus as our everything, the One who meets our every need and the needs of those He trusts us with. As we bow in absolute dependence, hindrances to a thriving relationship with Him come to light. Here, we discover that He is the solution, deliverer, and healer. He is miracle-working, transformational power. He is life and breath. He is unrelenting love.

When our interior life centers around Jesus and we become consumed with Him, trusting Him to be our strength, our perspective completely shifts. Suddenly, everything feels different. All internal complexities are bathed in divine truth, and inner peace and calm return. We begin to experience perfect love casting out all fear.

Trials aren't enjoyable, but they have the power to radically alter our perspective if our hearts are set on Christ. In the midst of the pain, we experience that He truly is all that we need. As we lean on our Beloved, He leads us into freedom. When we get ourselves off our mind, it catapults us into the longed-for place of victory. We see every situation bow to His Lordship, and the rule of the King is victoriously implemented in our hearts. We become compelled by love in all we do and say, as Jesus' strength becomes our own. His love surging through us is a motivating force. When our hearts are exhilarated, on fire with His desires, nothing else matters. We become pure expressions of the lovesick bride when we are compelled by love, despite temporary suffering.

My Heart's Response

Jesus, I am leaning on You, fully dependent on You. I want to be so consumed with love for You that no matter what I face, my heart continues to cry, "Holy, holy, holy!" Thank You for this unfolding revelation You are unveiling in the depths of my being. I don't like seasons of suffering, but I know that You are with me and will lead me to victory, even if it looks different than I expect. I trust You to work everything out for my good because I love You and I'm called according to Your purpose (see Romans 8:28).

Lord, in these difficult times, let my worship, my absolute and whole surrender, move Your heart and honor You. I hold nothing back. I want to be so in tune with You, so sensitized to our oneness and union, that I drip with Your Presence. I trust that out of these seasons of suffering love, You will give me treasures of breakthrough to share. I am so thankful to know that in each of these challenges, I will discover You as my true strength and watch as You bring beauty out of the ashes.

Day 25

Out of the Grave

Yes, God raised Jesus to life! And since God's Spirit of Resurrection lives in you, he will also raise your dying body to life by the same Spirit that breathes life into you!

Romans 8:11 TPT

One day, Jesus wrapped me from the bottom of my feet to the top of my head in brown-stained grave clothes that resembled an Egyptian mummy. When Jesus finished covering me with these grave clothes, He pulled a tip of the cloth and spun me very quickly, unraveling the bandages. Resurrection light and life began shooting out of me in every direction.

When I stopped spinning, I was in awe, totally overwhelmed. Jesus leaned toward me and gently touched my heart. He said, "I'm giving you My song, the sound of My life." Immediately, understanding flooded me and I knew that we were moving into a new place as the body of Christ.

All of us, not just a few forerunners, are going to express His life in us more comprehensively than ever before in history. The sound of who He is will become clear in our lives. We will be the very song of Jesus, which sounds like compassion, mercy, wisdom, patience, and grace.

Then Jesus said, "You're in the third day." I knew He was talking about walking in resurrection power. It's time to rejoice because the resurrection life of Christ in us is transforming us at a level that is beyond our comprehension. As we wholly surrender to Jesus, becoming saturated with His nature, we rise in resurrection power, shining for the world to see. It is our greatest honor to radiate with His light and draw others to Him.

My Heart's Response

Lord, You died to bring me into a relationship with You that is beyond compare. Following Your example, I lay my life down in exchange for Yours and submit every part of my being to You. Thank You that I am coming out of these grave clothes, shining with Your glory-light. I am rising in resurrection power, filled with the song of Your Spirit, releasing Your sound.

Thank You for this third-day invitation to stand in You and to shine, filled with the beauty and majesty of who You are, transforming me: body, soul, and spirit. Thank You for leading me into an awareness of how powerful I am because Your life is inside of me. I can do everything You lead me to do because I am not entwined with the things of this world but entirely absorbed by You. Now I will carry Your sound, fragrance, and life, so all may know the beauty of this love.

Day 26

Come Into My Rest

He offers a resting place for me in his luxurious love.
His tracks take me to an oasis of peace near the quiet brook of bliss.
Psalm 23:2 TPT

The Lord is inviting you to a new level of rest. Perhaps you've never known intimacy with Him that settles your heart into complete rest. If you aren't confident in the security of His love and still deal with anxiety or even a sense of unsettledness, God is releasing the answer of His love. Receive new grace to feel His Presence. Re-engage your heart as He draws you into a deeper place of perfect love that casts out all fear.

This is the season where every part of your heart is becoming healthy and whole, so at peace that you can sleep during the storm. Secure in His arms, resting on His chest, you will watch as He calms the storms in and around you. His grace will enable you to rest. This is the deep work happening in you now.

As you know Him more intimately, you will notice Him meeting every need of your heart, and your trust in Him will grow. This is His desire for you—to go deeper than you ever have and to live in the awareness of His wraparound love. Jesus wants you to experience His Presence every second. He longs for the reality of His love to lead you into a lifestyle of rest.

My Heart's Response

Yes, Lord! This is what I want, too. Thank You for being here with me right now, for pulling me into Your embrace, Your love melting away every trace of restlessness. I'm looking away from everything that has burdened my heart and made me feel anxious; I'm locking eyes with You. You are with me in this boat of life and You will keep me safe.

I feel the sweetness of Your love. The storm may still be raging but I am not afraid. Fear no longer holds a place in me because Your love leaves it no room. The awareness of Your Presence is becoming my continual reality. No matter what is happening around me, Your love has provided a foundation to stand on. Love has become my safe place, my home. From this place, where my entire life is wrapped up in You, I will live in peace. I will have rest in the deepest caverns of my soul.

Day 27

The King of Glory Within

A Prophetic Word

Living within you is the Christ who floods you with the expectation of glory! This mystery of Christ, embedded within us, becomes a heavenly treasure chest of hope filled with the riches of glory for his people, and God wants everyone to know it!

Colossians 1:7 TPT

The Lord says, "I am calling you forth. I am calling you forth into life. I'm calling you forth. Live, live, live!"

The King of Glory is in the center of your being, expanding within and filling you. He's creating an exact match between His body and your physical expression. His arms are slotted through your arms, His hands through your hands, fingers through your fingers. Feel Him right now. His legs are going down through your legs, His feet are fastening to yours. He fits Himself perfectly within you. You are one with Christ.

No matter how unqualified or weak you've felt, His supreme life is rising through you, strengthening you. The divine strength of the King will be noticeable now. The enemy will not succeed in his attacks against your life because the King is here! The radiant One has come.

The stature of the King is becoming visible through His body in the earth. When you lift your hands into the atmosphere, lay them on the sick, or on yourself, divine light shoots from the King's hands, out through yours. This holy oneness is becoming evident in your life. Unstoppable, recreative power is shooting through you. It is His divine light, His living power. Come forth, beautiful one! The King of Glory is in your midst.

My Heart's Response

Yes, Jesus, this is what I desire! To become more aware of You in me than I am of myself and my supposed limitations. Thank You for filling me and reminding me of the power of Your life inside of me. I am becoming aware of the greatness of what I carry within me, and I will never be the same.

I hear Your invitation to walk as a dispenser of Your glory in the earth. To rise in confidence and take You at Your word. I am rising up with You so that my life glorifies You. I will not be distracted by the doubts and fears that once plagued me. I am a home for the King of Glory. All of Your light, power, love, and authority are fully manifesting in and through me.

Day 28

His Dream for You

So let all who are fully mature have this same passion, and if anyone is not yet gripped by these desires, God will reveal it to them. And let us all advance together to reach this victory-prize, following one path with one passion.

Philippians 3:15-16 TPT

The Lord dreams that you would know His heart. Your heart and His, thriving in beautiful unity, face-to-face communion, flowing in a dance, rising as a song. Oh, that Jesus would always and forever remain your magnificent obsession. That you would know the unshakable fulfillment of radical abandon to Him, and that you would understand the indescribable freedom of complete surrender.

The Father has formed you into a new creation. Your life is destined to be an expression of His glory—an outlet of overflowing love because of your surrendered heart. Every part of your life is coming under the influence of His redemptive power. When you go low, His glory radiates from you. As you remain in trust, He moves in power. When you relinquish control, the King of the Universe stands as the ultimate authority in your life so that principalities and powers bow. Those lying spirits back off when truth becomes a reality to your heart.

God's dream for you encompasses every area of your life and extends into eternity. Living in ever-deepening intimacy with Jesus washes your perspective on life. Peace, joy, freedom, and power become a normal way of living when your thoughts are entwined with His. Step into this invitation today.

My Heart's Response

Jesus, I want to know You. Every fiber of my being feels the power of this invitation. Thank You for reaching out to me with Your love and purpose over and over again. Your unrelenting love has left me undone. Your kindness overwhelms me. Make Your dreams my reality.

I lay my life before You again. My heart is surrendered and open to Your transforming power. You are washing me with waves of glory and every cell is receiving new life, new light. It is no longer I who live, but it is You, Jesus, who lives through me. I reach for Your extended hand and step into this divine dance of freedom, love, and joy. I will live each day in our holy union, eyes glued to Yours, growing in this grace. Your life is surging into me, refining me, and now my thoughts, perceptions, words, and dreams are becoming a pure reflection of Yours.

Day 29

Love is Transforming You

We are being transfigured into his very image as we move from one brighter level of glory to another. And this glorious transfiguration comes from the Lord, who is the Spirit.

2 Corinthians 3:18 TPT

The wisest and most powerful thing that we can do, is to prioritize a heart-to-heart connection with Jesus. This is where breakthrough happens. This is the place where life-altering power surges into our souls. When we spend time in the secret place of His Presence, listening, worshiping, reading the Word, and focusing our attention on Him, we are changed.

Being with the Lord affects every single area of our lives. We have existed in Him before the beginning of time and this is where we continue to thrive. We were created and birthed from the womb of His love. In Him, inside the very essence of who He is, is everything we need for life and true identity.

Scripture says that every unfolding revelation transforms us. Sitting at His feet, listening and waiting with expectation, fine-tunes us. We often say that we want Jesus to change us. This is where that change happens—in the glory of His Presence. As we get to know the Lord more and more, seeing the different facets of His beauty, wisdom, and power, we are shifted into a new way of life. We are transformed from one degree of glory to the next, by soaking in His love. His Presence releases truth that, if settled in our hearts, revolutionizes our lives until we scarcely recognize ourselves.

My Heart's Response

Lord, thank You for infusing me with the fragrance of Your desire for my life. You have such glory waiting for me—greater revelation than my mind can conceive, more significant transformation than I know is possible. Yes, I want to see, to hear, to live with my heart glued to Yours. You are literally everything I need, and I never want to live outside of this reality.

You are my treasure, and I am Yours. It's mind-boggling to imagine how much You love me, but this truth is finally expanding inside of me. Your love is freeing me from the lies that have plagued my heart. The unfolding revelation of who You are is awakening my sleeping heart. Doubts are drowning in the ocean of deep encounters with You. I am becoming the bride You have always known I would be. Your love is transforming me.

Day 30

The Power of His Kiss

Let him smother me with kisses—his Spirit-kiss divine.
So kind are your caresses,
I drink them in like the sweetest wine!
Song of Songs 1:2 TPT

Jesus came and gently kissed the top of my head. This kiss is for you today. He is ravishing your heart, wrecking false narratives that you have believed, and awakening you to a new way of life. As you receive a fresh revelation of your Bridegroom King, Almighty God, tender Father, or however He chooses to reveal Himself to you, it lands on your heart like a kiss.

Nothing compares to the exhilarating experience of feeling the love of Jesus. The fresh infusion of who He is, is moving into you with life-transforming strength just by receiving His kiss. One of the meanings of the word 'kiss' ('nashaq' in Hebrew) is 'to be equipped with weapons'. The intimate kiss of the Lord strengthens you, providing you with all that you need to stand in His absolute and ultimate authority. His love produces a warrior capacity inside of you.

Like the Shulamite, when you come out of the wilderness, leaning on your Beloved, utterly abandoned and surrendered to Jesus, it enables you to tap into His undefeatable strength. Unflinchingly secure in His love, you become courageous, absolutely convinced of who He is in you. As you stand in your oneness with the King, you whisper His decrees and see His purposes come to pass in the earth. This is the power of His kiss.

My Heart's Response

Jesus, I'm awestruck over the power Your kiss has had in my life and the power it is continuing to release. Intimacy with You is strengthening me and giving me the courage to stand as Your confident bride. Thank You for wrapping me with Your love, and holding me close when the wilderness felt like it was stripping me bare.

My walk is becoming steady and victorious because I am living in the reality of this kiss. So kiss me, over and over again, until my heart cannot be moved by doubt or fear. Your love is my joy! I am learning to live in my identity as the bride, who rules and reigns with You. My prayers are powerful because they flow from Your heart. My touch releases healing and miracles because it is done in agreement with Your Word. Your kiss has equipped me for battle.

Day 31

The Power of Abiding

Because I set you, Yahweh, always close to me,
my confidence will never be weakened,
for I experience your wraparound Presence every moment.
Psalm 16:8 TPT

Jesus is inviting us to live in constant awareness of His abiding Presence. For too long, we've jumped from spirit to soul and back again—one moment enjoying Him and the next moment feeling stressed and overwhelmed. We have been welcomed into a life of union with no sense of separation, yet we've settled for intermittent encounters. The Lord longs for us to remain attentive to our oneness, sensitized to and resting in the arms of His indwelling Presence. Yes, we've cried out for this and longed for it, but now it is time to walk in it.

It starts with our surrendered will, letting go, and embracing the glorious Christ within. Choosing to believe in the absolute power of our God, in His perfect leadership and faithfulness, and the price Jesus paid for us to live in union with Him, is what ignites our faith. Being utterly convinced of His love for us is what makes faith effortless. The moment distraction comes and tempts us to fear, we tune into the Prince of Peace living within us, and peace increases.

When the enemy baits us, we immediately recognize the lie and turn to the One who is the truth. When we are fully secure in God's love, our hearts will flourish, repelling the darkness that once consumed our thoughts. We will rule and reign with Christ when we remain in tune with His Spirit.

My Heart's Response

Jesus, thank You for reframing my thoughts with truth. You have called me to live a life that is fully engaged with the Kingdom of heaven, instead of constantly distracted by the cares of this world. I don't want to go in and out, up and down, one second standing in faith and the next moment leaning on my own understanding. Today, I come into agreement with truth.

All that You are—perfect love, faithfulness, majesty, wisdom, creative power, mercy, and might, has its home inside of me. You have not left me helpless. You are my ever-present help, the One who loves me. You are my faithful Shepherd, who leads and guides me by Your eye. Thank You for teaching me to live in the awareness of our oneness. Although the temptation to forget this truth may knock on my door, You've already granted me the victory. I am learning to enjoy the joy of abiding, by embracing the beauty of surrender.

Day 32

Freedom Belongs to You

And I find that the strength of Christ's explosive power infuses me to conquer every difficulty.

Philippians 4:13 TPT

Anything that isn't in Christ's character doesn't belong in us. Jesus is not depressed, He's not oppressed, and He's not full of anxiety and fear. The Lord understands the earth-walk, and He never condemns us for our feelings or shames us for what we go through, but He longs for us to receive freedom. When we lean into Holy Spirit, He speaks to our hearts and shows us how to walk in victory. We are called to co-create with God, listening to His wisdom so that we can declare and decree His desires over our lives.

When we connect to our true identity in Christ, and nothing defines us other than Jesus, our hearts come alive to life-transforming truth. He is taking us deeper, revealing the power of our entwined lives so that we live in freedom. This is the next level, where we refuse to accept anything in our spirit, mind, emotions, or body that doesn't reflect Jesus.

Today, the Lord is highlighting stress, anxiety, depression, or any emotional or psychological condition resulting from warfare. These things can't remain when our hearts have fully woken up to the power of Christ inside of us. If anything in you does not reflect the perfection of who you are in Christ, speak His truth to those areas.

My Heart's Response

Jesus, I come into agreement with Your will for my life. Anything I've believed that isn't consistent with Your truth, isn't mine. If it isn't in Your nature, it doesn't belong to me! Thank You for defining my identity, for reminding me that I can live in freedom no matter my current condition or what my past was like. You are Lord of every area.

By faith, I declare my day of deliverance! I am one with the very Person of breakthrough. I bow my thoughts to none other than the Prince of Peace. The Holy Spirit, who raised Christ from the dead, dwells inside of me. I am powerful, peaceful, healed, and whole in every area. I am free from despair, free from loneliness. Nothing can separate me from Your love. Every provision for my life has already been granted, and I am coming into victory now.

Day 33

I Am Your Freedom

A Prophetic Word

But those who wait for the Lord [who expect, look for, and hope in Him]
Will gain new strength and renew their power;
They will lift up their wings [and rise up close to God] like eagles [rising toward the sun]...
Isaiah 40:31 AMP

Close your eyes and sit with Me. I am releasing the grace for another level of freedom. I am escorting fear from the stage of your life. As we advance, there will be no place for fear. I created you to live in joy and freedom.

I've watched you struggle, dragging weights you weren't meant to wear—heavy chains of restriction. The enemy thought he could slip a harness of slavery around your mind, but I have paid the price for your deliverance. I am here, beloved, and I am unchaining you from the lies that fear has bound you with. You don't have to work to make this happen, just look at Me. I am your freedom.

Heaviness is melting off of you right now. Breathe the fresh air of a new day. The inheritance of the Gospel is this—all you need, I have provided. I freed you and I'm strengthening you. This is the grace of your oneness with Me. I am all that you need. Entwine with Me. Come with Me to the brooks of bliss; look into it, and you will see both of our faces reflecting off the water. You are My mirror image. In this place of freedom, all that I am is all that you are in the world.

My Heart's Response

Lord, thank You for this grace You're dispensing. As I wait upon You and entwine my heart with Yours, my thoughts finally settle down and I can hear You. The power of Your words resonates deep within my spirit, and I can feel the life they're releasing inside of me. I feel myself being transformed by everything You've said. I am being changed into something very different than I was before. I am becoming who I was created to be.

In the cocoon of your Presence, Your love is washing and freeing me. I feel lighter. The heaviness and restrictions that plagued me have fallen off. I'm bathed in the oil of Your glory, making it impossible for the lies to stick to me. In Your mercy, You're scrubbing away even the tiniest fragment of fear and distrust, and I'm emerging in Your image. I'm glistening with the beauty of who You are.

Day 34

Be Still and Know

Surrender your anxiety.
Be still and realize that I am God.
I am God above all the nations,
and I am exalted throughout the whole earth.
Psalm 46:10 TPT

The Lord wants to take you into a new understanding of His heart for you. He's pouring out a new revelation of who He is so that you can know Him more intimately than you ever have before. So, sink deep into His love and relinquish control. Just let go. Settle into His arms, into the arms of the Person of grace inside of you. Let go of the responsibilities and pressure for just a moment. Set your gaze on Jesus and open your heart to the Lord. You're safe with Him.

The One who is the solution is here. Your miracle-working, promise-keeping God is with you to bring you into utter freedom and rest. His Presence is filling the atmosphere around and in you. His peace is quieting your thoughts. God's glory is realigning you at your very core. He is setting you free from burdens you weren't meant to carry. For those who are burned out, stagnant, and feel spiritually dull, His love is exhilarating you again.

Lean in, and you will sense His nearness. You can hear and feel Him! Anything that told you otherwise is a lie, and Holy Spirit is freeing you from that lie right now. Stay in this place for as long as you're able. Rest in this love for a while. Be still and know that He is God. He is for you, and He has come to be with you today.

My Heart's Response

Jesus, thank You for releasing the fresh breath of Your life into me. Heaviness is melting away as I let go and rest with You. I feel the shift. Thank You for coming as You promised that You would. You are drawing me into another level of Your Presence, more real and profound than I've ever known.

From this moment forward, I will never be the same. Every pathway in my mind is being washed in Your holy blood. I can think clearly now because my thoughts are aligned with Yours. Weariness has lost its grip. A settled joy that can only come from You is strengthening me. Fresh hope and faith are rising from deep within. I feel my heart being reset as You free me from every burden. I am still and steady on the inside because You are here.

Day 35

Unshakable Confidence in Him

Arise, my love.
Open your heart, my darling, deeper still to me.
Will you receive me this dark night?
There is no one else but you, my friend, my equal.
Song of Songs 5:2 TPT

We are coming into a new day, where we will live in absolute confidence in who we are and in our God-given destiny. It is starting now, as we wholeheartedly surrender, laying our lives down in exchange for His. When every desire bows to Jesus, we connect to the One within us in a new way. Undistracted by our own will, we press in to hear Him, longing to know the intentions of His heart. As we prioritize time with Jesus and begin to understand our true identity, we're rising as His confident bride. We are becoming consumed with the Lord and it is changing everything.

True to your identity, sure of who you are in Christ, completely yielded to Him in every way, you are being entrusted with His heart. Despite the darkness covering the earth, you will shine with His light. You will speak forth His will in absolute confidence because you know His desire. This is what happens to lovesick hearts who know their God. See yourself standing in this mystery today.

Embrace the call to co-reign with Him, carrying His authority everywhere you go. You are being transformed and are emerging as the beautiful, confident bride that He knew you would be.

My Heart's Response

Lord, thank You for washing my soul from doubt. Help me not to look at myself when situations arise that require miracles that only You can give. I don't want to hold back when You ask me to take bold steps. I bow before You and lay my will, pride, and fears at Your feet. You have called me to live in Your perfect love that casts out fear. Thank You for the power of that truth.

I submit myself to You and declare that a fear of looking foolish will not dictate my obedience. I don't need to impress anyone because this isn't about me; it's about You. I will no longer dim the light shining in me because of doubt. I am absolutely, entirely Yours, and I believe in Your glory inside of me. I don't care how I look to anyone but You. Our love is my only motivation. It is my honor to walk with Your authority. Thank You for dispensing fresh faith within me today and for trusting me with Your heart.

Day 36

Release His Light

Darkness blankets the earth,
and thick gloom covers the nations,
but Yahweh arises upon you
and the brightness of his glory appears over you!
Nations will be attracted to your radiant light...
Isaiah 60:2-3 TPT

The Lord is revealing areas of our hearts that don't look or sound like Him. He has heard our prayers and in response, has come to transform us. He is intervening to set us free from self-focus, compromise, and limiting beliefs. We have longed to walk in the fullness of His promises, so He has come to show us everything that hinders us from the fulfillment of that desire. Jesus is coming for a bride without blemish or wrinkle, a radiant bride who shines with the light of His glory into a dark and weary world.

This is what happens when we fully submit to Him—we shine with the brightness of His glory. When we take on God's nature, walking in His love, compassion, kindness, wisdom, and peace, nations are attracted to what we carry. All the world will know that we are His. Christ's nature will flow from us like a sweet fragrance.

His light will emanate from us, bathing the nations with His Presence. We will release peace into chaos and healing will follow us. Jesus partners with His fully yielded, love-sick bride to manifest the restoration of all things. We are here at the perfect time in history, it is our time to shine.

My Heart's Response

Lord, thank You for exposing soulish distractions that keep me from shining brightly. You illuminate every area of my life that doesn't reflect You, and I am so grateful. Walking in the fullness of who You are inside of me is my desire. I want to look and sound like You in every way, living from the strength of my union with You continually. I relinquish control and lean into Your sovereignty, yielding to Your Spirit within me and choosing to trust You completely.

Now Your desires are becoming my own. I am stepping into my rightful place. The fruit of Your Spirit is on display in my life, testifying of Your great love. My words are seasoned with grace. My hands flow with Your healing oil. Your nature is my nature, I am learning to live as a new creation. I am saturated with You, fully immersed in the awareness of our oneness. I am becoming the bride that You have always dreamed I would be. Together, we're releasing light into the darkness.

Day 37

Your Most Beautiful Gift

Listen, my dearest darling,
you are so beautiful—you are beauty itself to me!
Your eyes are
like gentle doves behind your veil.
What devotion I see each time I gaze upon you.
Song of Songs 4:1 TPT

One day, while worshiping, I found myself in heaven. There was no consciousness of the natural realm. I was entirely there, and I was terrified. I stood in an enormous throne room, overwhelmed by my surroundings, unable to move. I was glued to the spot, frozen in awe. I felt like a little girl dressed in rags. The moment I saw Jesus, my heart felt like it would burst. I immediately lost all self-consciousness. I was undone, unglued, and totally free. There are no inhibitions in the atmosphere of heaven. We're free to be the full expression of how He created us.

I began sobbing and crying, "I love You, Jesus! I love You, Jesus!" It wasn't a pretty expression of worship; I was uncontrollably screaming my love. In response, Jesus leaned in close. I reached up to touch His face, and all of heaven fell silent. The entirety of His attention was focused on me as He drank in my authentic love. Heaven honored this precious moment when Jesus received the reward of His suffering: my messy, ugly explosion of love-drenched tears and screaming.

Your authentic love, no matter how weak or compromised you may feel, moves Jesus and as He savors it, heaven goes silent. Whether it's a whisper or a scream, He cherishes your outpouring of genuine love. Your heart's cry, this flood of undiluted worship, is His reward. You are an exquisite experience of love to His heart.

My Heart's Response

Jesus, You are the most-beautiful One! I'm overwhelmed and completely undone hearing how You delight in my love. I have no words to describe this love that swells within me, to know that You treasure my love for You even in my weakness, it has taken me over. This holy devotion has become my entire life, and I will not withhold it from You.

My every breath declares my absolute surrender. I am Yours. Although words fail to describe the depth of my passion and appreciation, I pour them out to bless You, to thrill You the way that You have thrilled me. Thank You for accepting my love. Though it seems inadequate to me, You delight in it. So, enjoy it. Drink it. Savor it, Lord, for my devotion is genuine.

Day 38

Light Dispels All Darkness

Then Jesus said, "I am light to the world,
and those who embrace me will experience life-giving light,
and they will never walk in darkness."
John 8:12 TPT

You have been brought into the Kingdom of light where darkness cannot exist. It is in this light that true freedom, deliverance, and breakthrough manifest. As a child of the King, you are one with His Spirit, one with the glory that dispels all darkness that opposes you. You have been given a gift that no power can steal. The Lord sanctioned your freedom and chiseled it into your heart. No evil can steal it away. It cannot maintain a grip on your life when you're walking in your oneness with Jesus. Tune into the truth of this unimaginable power.

This power, this union with light Himself, has made you into an entirely new creation. Light and love have transformed you and changed the substance of who you are. His love opened the door to an entirely new way of life. The old you has died.

When Jesus holds the only place of influence in your life, the enemy has no legal ground to steal what is rightfully yours. You have the same authority to dispel the darkness that Jesus does because He is in you. Your agreement with these truths brings your heart into alignment with His. You can live in the strength of this truth every day.

My Heart's Response

Lord, I detach from worldly weights and soulish distractions. These dark shadows of doubt, fear, and unbelief are not meant to influence me. I am a child of light. Thank You that as I abide in the awareness of You inside of me, I am changed from glory to glory. In this light, I am delivered from darkness. In You, I see the truth.

Thank You for this freedom to live a life of peace and power. Thank You for these revelations and face-to-face encounters where I see my true nature reflected in Your eyes. I'm becoming aware of the unimaginable glory You have infused within me. I am one with You. I am powerful because the Source of all power is in me. You are aligning me with truth and I will not agree with any other opinion. I am walking in the light of that truth now, and darkness has no claim on my life. Your glory is framing my reality.

Day 39

Let the ‘Pauls’ Arise

A Prophetic Word

...and I heard a voice saying to me in Hebrew, ‘Saul, Saul, why are you persecuting me? It is not for you to kick against your own conscience.’ ‘Who are you, Lord?’ I said. And the Lord said to me, ‘I am Jesus whom you are persecuting. Now get up and stand on your feet for I have shown myself to you for a reason...

Acts 26:14-16 J. B. Phillips

Jesus drew my attention to this scripture and said, “Paul’s blood cries out. Many will now meet me on their Damascus Road.” Heaven is calling in divine recompense for Paul's murder. Leaders worldwide are about to be interrupted on their journey to enact laws that persecute Christians and damage humanity. They’re about to be met by Jesus.

There is going to be a harvest of ‘Pauls’. Jesus is asking us to pray and call them forth from across nations, from a myriad of expressions of life. Some hidden from view, some very visible, all deceived. The Lord is bringing them out of the gross deception that has held them. Many will come forth as global evangelists. They will be rough diamonds who will look messy as their character is being purified, but they will love Jesus with a holy passion in response to His great love and mercy.

They will walk in awe of God as messengers of power: yielded, sold-out, and uncompromising in their faith. They will walk like Paul, and they are coming home now! Then the Lord said, "Satan has had his day. This is part of heaven's great mercy and divine strategy that is unleashing now; to turn the nations from darkness into light."

My Heart's Response

Lord, Your mercy and compassion amaze me. You love so fiercely and purely, and I'm reminded that this is how You have called me to walk. Thank You for teaching and leading me on this path of mercy. Even in judgment, You love. Help me to do the same. Enable me to see others through Your eyes and remember that You died for those who persecuted You.

I too choose to forgive those who have aligned themselves with satan's agenda. Let the 'Sauls' be radically changed by Your mercy. Reveal Yourself to them and set them free. Ignite a holy passion in them that sets the world ablaze!

Lord, I avail myself to You. Shine Your glory through me as I meet those who have been deceived, so they may be enlightened by the truth that sets men free. Let the world changers arise!

Day 40

Releasing Words of Life

Out of the same mouth come both blessing and cursing. These things, my brothers, should not be this way [for we have a moral obligation to speak in a manner that reflects our fear of God and profound respect for His precepts].

James 3:10 AMP

Our words contain creative power. Through our speech, we can build up or we can tear down. We can heal a soul or inflict a wound, we can create connection or cause division. What we say reveals what's in our hearts. The quality of our life is influenced by our speech and framed by our beliefs. When we live in agreement with heaven, we become a sound of love.

If you struggle with gossip, find yourself speaking cutting, judgmental words, or words that don't carry Jesus' heart, this is your moment to step into freedom. Your speech is the overflow of what is in your heart. So, if you realize that your words are filled with doubt, anger, fear, resentment, etc. invite the Lord to get to the root of these things so that you can be free.

It's so important that the atmosphere encircling us is infused with heaven. We want to live as representatives on earth, revealing the culture of our Kingdom home. It is a beautiful thing when we live in kindness, releasing grace, mercy, and love. It's important that we are aware of what we say, but it's more important to get to the heart of the matter and be healed in the areas that cause these flippant, lifeless words to manifest.

My Heart's Response

Jesus, thank You for bringing this to the light. I want every part of my being to be fully aligned with You. Let Your blood wash away the impurities that reveal themselves through my speech. Thank You that this is a new day for me. Thank You for setting me free from this struggle and causing my heart now to be fully in sync with Yours.

Saturate me in Your love and heal the soul wounds, evidenced by what I say. Season my speech with love, grace, and compassion. I will tune into Your heart for others so that I can be a safe place where people feel and hear only You. Heal any relationships I've injured. I give You my heart and ask that You would be Lord of every word. Jesus, thank You for bringing this shift and freedom into my heart today.

Day 41

Baptized in Love

For we've been buried with him into his death. Our "baptism into death" also means we were raised with him when we believed in God's resurrection power, the power that raised him from death's realm.
Colossians 2:12 TPT

The invitation to a life of power, peace, wisdom, and joy is extended to every Believer. Jesus is encouraging us to step into our new life in Him, completely. He is welcoming us into the joys of supernatural living, of resurrection life. But before every resurrection, there is first a death.

When Jesus died on the Cross, He took us with Him. Love compelled Jesus to lay everything down so that He would be raised in the victory He shares with us. It was for the joy set before Him that He endured the Cross. This love we now experience, this joy of being fully one with Jesus, is the strength of our life. When we recognize that we no longer live but Christ lives in us, that we are a completely new creation, our entire existence changes.

This ultimate baptism of love is where we emerge in His resurrection power. Because of love, we let go of everything that doesn't look like Jesus so that we can rise with His nature. Now, we live in the power and purity of who He created us to be, influenced by nothing other than the Spirit of God inside of us. Love is awakening us to our true identity. Love is becoming the primary motivation of our life. There is nothing off-limits now because we're completely surrendered to Him. This is the secret of divine life, where we're compelled and motivated by the supernatural love of God in all things.

My Heart's Response

Jesus, thank You for nurturing my heart with the truth of who I am in You, for reminding me that resurrection power surges in and through me. I desire to live from this place of abiding, of oneness, and to thrive daily in the place of ecstatic love. I invite You to take over and live in me with exceeding greatness.

For the joy set before me—the pleasure of our absolute inseparability, I lay everything down, just as You did. And now, I am rising in Your power. My heart is flourishing with the truth of who You are. Every facet of Your nature is unfolding as revelation to my heart and infusing me with divine life. Thank You that the reality of the finished work of the Cross is awakening in me.

Day 42

Becoming Light

So don't hide your light! Let it shine brightly before others, so that your commendable works will shine as light upon them, and then they will give their praise to your Father in heaven.

Matthew 5:16 TPT

Live in the light of Jesus' countenance, your heart entwined with His, and you will become light. You will take stock of your life, your faith, your responses to trials, and realize that the darkness is gone. It has simply vanished and there isn't a shadow of doubt.

When you look at yourself, you will be amazed—you look like Jesus. There's a brightness to you that wasn't there before. You behave and sound just like the One you're beholding. The atmosphere around you is filling with light and faith that repels the enemy; he cannot remain where there is no agreement with his lies. When you're connected to the glory within you, the enemy backs off. This is the place of victorious warfare. Living in this face-to-face reality stirs a settled peace that effortlessly dispels darkness.

The glory of this faith stance is that it glorifies Jesus. When we walk in the light and it seeps from every cell—through love, patience, peace, compassion, and miraculous power, people will know that we belong to the Lord. When our lives are entirely integrated with the Spirit's, agape love will beam from everything we say and do. We will live in power, bringing heaven to earth everywhere we go and Jesus will be glorified. Jesus is life and light, and when we soak in His Presence, we are being absorbed into that light where darkness ceases to exist. We are becoming one with Light Himself.

My Heart's Response

Lord, bathe me in Your glory. With Your perfect love, wash away the shadows that still have a grip on my soul. I come into agreement with truth and light. I sink into Your arms and turn my eyes from the darkness that has fought to capture my attention. Thank You for resetting my heart and illuminating the gateway of my faith. King of Glory, flow through me.

This is where I choose to live now—in the continual awareness of love, undistracted by any other voice. King of Glory, flow into me and through me with Your splendor. Shine on my path and lead my every step. I am becoming like You—beautiful and radiant, dispersing darkness as we walk together. The victory of my life will be that You are continually glorified.

Day 43

Jesus is Restoring You

For the Lord God is a Sun and Shield; the Lord bestows [present] grace and favor and [future] glory (honor, splendor, and heavenly bliss)! No good thing will He withhold from those who walk uprightly.
Psalm 84:11 AMPC

Open your heart to the Lord and relax. Just let go and choose to become aware of His magnificent beauty. He is with you right now, and He wants you to experience His love more profoundly than you ever have. There is always more, always deeper realms of glory to explore. Jesus wants you to be totally and completely free in every area. That is His desire for you today—to set you free in the presence of His relentless love.

No area of your soul is off-limits. No mental turmoil or physical battle is beyond His reach. He wants you to be healthy and whole, even more than you want to be, and He's already paid the price for this to happen. As you rest in the Presence of Jesus, He is healing and reestablishing you. He is taking the heavy burdens that you willingly relinquish. This is what He does.

You can't dwell in the beauty of God's manifest glory and not be touched by Him. His very being drips with pure love, power, truth, and glory. Just as we read in the Gospels: He heals the sick, raises the dead, cleanses the lepers, and casts out demons. Through His death and resurrection, Jesus restored His beloved creation to its original design and intent. That is what He is doing for you today.

My Heart's Response

Jesus, when I reflect on the glory of Your love, I'm overwhelmed. You have so faithfully ministered to me and have already given me so many victories. Thank You for restoring me and healing me in the deep caverns of my soul, where pain once dictated my reality. You are restoring me and reframing my identity with Your own.

I feel You reaching into the depths of my heart and pouring Your liquid love into every cell. You're teaching me that I am royalty, that I am loved, and I am Your dream. No longer do I need to fight to survive because I am secure and confident in Your love. I trust the truth of healing. I know the power of Your Spirit inside of me. My heart is coming alive, and I will live in the reality of Your love and faithfulness forever.

Day 44

Living in Glory-Light

Revive us, O God! Let your beaming face shine upon us with the sunrise rays of glory;
then nothing will be able to stop us.
Psalm 80:3 TPT

As I share this encounter, engage the Lord. Open your heart to Jesus and expect Him to impart revelation. Taste and see. Drink of His Presence. Let today's devotion be a doorway to your own encounter with Him.

Jesus took me to the Father. I was in front of Him and I was terrified. I turned and entered a place of darkness, and when I did, I became a pillar of light. A triple helix of the Father's DNA swirled in and through me with glory-light. The fear of God gripped me. Almighty God was purifying my being, transfiguring me, completing me with His own DNA. Suddenly, I understood that I was tasting the future reality of the completion of the bride.

We are those who are called to live in the temple of our God, to stand in the glory of heaven while on a darkened earth. The earth is groaning for the bondage of decay to be broken. As sons, as brides, we are meant to release light into the darkness. We are called to release the sound of heaven into the chaos. To continually exist in the reality of

God's glory instead of popping in and out. To confidently stand in our identity as pillars of His light, by shining Him into the world through our words, actions, and heart-beliefs.

My Heart's Response

Lord, thank You for realigning me with Your perfect nature. I lay every false identity at Your feet. I lift my head and heart to You and submit afresh. King of Glory, come and fill every inch of me with Your holy DNA. Wash my mind with brilliant hues of cleansing light. I see it now, cascading like golden rivers of living water over every cell. You are awakening me to who I really am.

Jesus, thank You for pouring this revelation into me repeatedly. I cherish what You're teaching me and I'm absorbing it deep into my being. The Light of the world is inside of me. I am one with You and I will walk in the unfolding revelation of this truth for the rest of my life. Though I stand in the midst of darkness, I will shine with You.

Day 45

You Are Enough

A Prophetic Word

Then you will be empowered to discover what every holy one experiences—the great magnitude of the astonishing love of Christ in all its dimensions. How deeply intimate and far-reaching is his love! How enduring and inclusive it is!

Ephesians 3:18 TPT

Where your life has felt void of the true expression of who you are, where your emotions and soul have been parched, Jesus is saturating you with Himself. Where you've been spiritually dehydrated and where demons have gripped your mind, Jesus is releasing the divine light of the great I AM. The King has risen up. He has risen on your behalf. He's heard your cries and He has risen up.

Though the enemy confused you, Jesus is smashing the deception. He is demolishing those lies that said you weren't holy enough, good enough, important enough, or that you couldn't be loved. Some of you have strived to be something more so that He would love and accept you. But He already loves you. He accepted and drew you to Himself when He hung on that Cross.

There is nothing more to do, other than accept this truth and live in the bliss of holy union, fully surrendered to Him. See Jesus looking you in the eyes as He says, “You are My dream come true. You’re not a disappointment. I love you just as you are. Fix your eyes on Me and I’ll heal you, refresh you, and transform you. Let Me do the work in your beautiful, surrendered heart. I’ve got you. You’re safe with Me. I’m right here.”

My Heart's Response

Jesus, thank You that You are unveiling greater truth within me. You're doing it right now. Right now, You’re unveiling within me the unlimited riches of Your glory and favor. Supernatural strength is flooding my innermost being—it’s Your divine might and explosive power. It is the unlimited riches of life with You, Jesus, and I receive it! Unfold the next revelation of who You are into my heart. Saturate me with Your glory.

By constantly using the gift of faith You have given me, Your life is released inside me. The resting place of Your love is becoming the very source and root of my life. I am being empowered to discover what every holy one experiences—the great magnitude of the astonishing love that You have for me, in all its dimensions.

Day 46

Living in Union

Remain in Me, and I [will remain] in you.
John 15:4 AMP

The Father is calling us to abide in the garden of His heart. He longs for us to experience the bliss of His love, the knowledge of His will, and the blessing of His wisdom in an ongoing way. The days of moving in and out of His Presence are behind us, and we are stepping into the gift of union with Christ. This is an unfathomable blessing. This is God's will—that we would remain in unbroken communion with Him, to live spirit to Spirit, continually.

You have been invited to dwell in the Presence of the King, to remain in Him, to be taught daily by the Spirit who is moving inside of you. If you make the Lord your heart's priority and set your daily affection on Him, He will align you; spirit, soul, and body. The appeal from heaven is to connect and become so fully, consistently conscious, so absolutely consumed with the Spirit of God, that every part of your being is transfigured with light.

Perfection, wholeness, and health in every area manifest as you live consciously beholding Almighty God. He is the Wisdom of the Ages. Jesus is the doorway that is open before you. Step in. Make the Lord's

Presence your dwelling place and the troubles of this world will grow strangely dim.

My Heart's Response

Jesus, You're so glorious! Thank You for allowing me the honor of abiding in You. Holy Spirit, consume every distraction that tries to entice me. I desire to live in this place of continual interaction with You. I don't want anything to dilute my awareness of our holy union. So, I let go of soulish entanglements that bear no spiritual fruit. I want my life to testify of You.

Temporary trials will not silence my desire for You. I will not try to reason my way out of difficulties, instead, I will lock eyes with You. I will tune into the glories of heaven and hear what You have to say. You are causing my spirit and soul to live in agreement with Your Spirit. Your Presence is my joy. Regardless of the chaos rumbling around me, I will choose to remember You. I will stand with an unbroken gaze and declare that You alone are holy.

Day 47

Lovers Reign

...There is no one else but you, my friend, my equal.
I need you this night to arise and come be with me.
You are my pure, loyal dove, a perfect partner for me.
My flawless one, will you arise?
Song of Songs 5:2 TPT

We are being transformed into the image of our Bridegroom King. Through our intimacy with Him, our hearts are awakening; remembering as we behold and are filled with the attributes and nature of God. When we spend time with the Lord, cherishing the truths He reveals and living in awareness of our holy union, we start looking and sounding more like Jesus.

We are becoming the bride He always dreamed that we would be. We are becoming more acquainted with His desires, and it is our great honor to reveal them to the world around us. Our love relationship with Jesus is creating confidence in us to stand as His representatives on the earth.

To use the language of royalty, the queen stands alongside the king, operating in absolute, governmental, majestic authority; lovers reign together. They trust each other and work in harmony to advance the kingdom in which they rule. Jesus has called us to reign with Him, starting now and into eternity. We are meant to partner with Him for the restoration and fulfillment of all things, to release the Kingdom of heaven everywhere we go, to display the beauty, sovereignty, power, perfection, and wisdom of God.

He has chosen to do this through us, with us, and from within us. But for His dream to become reality, we must believe in who we are. We must take this message to heart and believe that we are who He says we are. We are royalty.

My Heart's Response

Jesus, I am awestruck by this revelation. At times I feel insignificant and unworthy, totally unsuitable for such a role. But You reveal Your heart to me with ceaseless patience. You want me to shake off doubt and engage Your truth, to shut my eyes to what seems evident in the natural and open myself to an eternal reality.

Thank You for redeeming me, for beautifying me with Your Spirit, and making me holy so that I have permission to stand with You, my majestic King. Thank You for calling me to reign alongside You; extending the scepter of authority and entrusting me with it. Knowing Your heart, and releasing the reality of Your power and love into the earth is an honor I do not take for granted.

Day 48

The Ongoing Experience of Love

You will keep in perfect and constant peace the one whose mind is steadfast [that is, committed and focused on You—in both inclination and character],
Because he trusts and takes refuge in You [with hope and confident expectation].
Isaiah 26:3 AMP

The enemy's objective is to block us from God's glory. He works to desensitize us and keep us busy. He wants us to be riddled with bondages and impaired by brokenness and disassociation. If he can sit at the gate of our souls so that we're consumed by our problems and forget who we are, then he prevents us from operating in our authority. But we can choose to whom we yield. We can decide which reality we agree with.

The grace of God is available to help us stay connected to Jesus in the depths of our hearts, even when our minds are tempted to succumb to fear, unbelief, and stress. Our lives are meant to be an experiential walk with Jesus, even during times of busyness, crises, or weariness. He wants us to remain aware of our union with God so that despite the things we go through, we are convinced that He hasn't left us.

When we believe in our unbroken connection with the Lord, we will not be easy prey for the enemy. We will stand strong in Christ and maintain a heavenly perspective when we live in an ongoing experience of His love. And this love will be like a power wash for our spirits and souls. Though our faith may be tried, we will emerge victorious. There is no trial strong enough to separate us from His love.

My Heart's Response

Jesus, my heart is set upon You. I have lived in a back and forth reality of Your Presence long enough. From this point on, by Your grace, I will remain at rest in Your love, tuned into Your heart. Thank You for calling me higher to live from the established place of my identity in You. I am becoming absolutely convinced of our oneness.

Because of this awareness of You inside of me, nothing comes between us. No trial separates me from You. Storms may rage but my soul is still. My mind is quiet, and I hear You whispering Your love and wisdom. I am being strengthened by Your love.

No matter what comes, my spirit remains drenched with Living Waters. Your Kingdom perspective is the only truth I will agree with. Fear no longer drags me along its path because Your love is establishing me. You have Your hand on every detail of my life.

Day 49

God is Flooding You

And provide for those who grieve in Zion—
to bestow on them a crown of beauty
instead of ashes,
the oil of joy
instead of mourning,
and a garment of praise
instead of a spirit of despair.
They will be called oaks of righteousness,
a planting of the Lord
for the display of his splendor.
Isaiah 61:3 NIV

I saw the Lord flowing like an overflowing, gushing well. He was moving with powerful force to expel the debris that has been blocking and restricting you. Receive this now. Jesus is dispensing the entirety of Himself throughout your whole being—body, soul, and spirit, to free you. The Spirit of God is flooding you with the surety of His glory. The power of God is flushing out the obstructions that have been piling up. The Comforter is comforting you. He is resetting you and reminding you how loved, cared for, and valuable you are.

Nothing can stop the intention of Jesus from manifesting in your life. He wants you to fully experience Him, to a greater degree than you ever have before. Engage your heart with His desire for your life. Love is shifting you into a new dimension of reality that contradicts natural reasoning.

As you walk in the light of His countenance, His perspective is becoming your own. Freedom is becoming your continual experience so that you can lead others into the same supernatural way of life. Faith is rising in you and demolishing what once restricted your forward movement in Christ. You will never be the same.

My Heart's Response

Jesus, I feel Your glory shining through my entire being. Darkness has lost its grip and is being completely eradicated by the power of Your unstoppable love; love that changes everything. Thank You for shifting my perspective so that it agrees with Yours. You are tuning me into the frequency of heaven and giving me wisdom. The restrictions that once hindered me from living in perfect peace no longer exist, they have been power washed in glory. From now on, every test and trial will only serve to drive me closer to You.

My soul bows to You. My thoughts are united to Yours and my heart is eternally connected to Yours. In this place of connection, I remain unblocked. Nothing can move me anymore. I am living in the power of our oneness, strong in our union, led only by Your Spirit. And this will be my testimony—Your perfect love has set me free. Your life in me has reframed my reality.

Day 50

Bathed in Light

A Prophetic Word

Look carefully! Darkness blankets the earth,
and thick gloom covers the nations,
but Yahweh arises upon you
and the brightness of his glory appears over you!
Isaiah 60:2 TPT

Today, total victory is being released to you. Where the enemy has assailed you, held you captive, tormented, intimidated, and oppressed you, Jesus is setting you free. He is exposing the lies of the evil one. You are not small and insignificant. The enemy is a liar! He has been exposed and today, Jesus is washing you with His radiant love. The enemy's work in your life is over! All ground that has become a playground for his manipulation and lies is being taken back by the Lord. He says, "No more!"

Angels are ministering to you. Things in the unseen realm that have restricted your movements, your breath, and your spiritual expression are being pulled off of you. Jesus is breaking it all off. He is setting you free! The light of Christ, His truth and love, are streaming from heaven straight into your heart. Light is driving out darkness, shame, self-condemnation, and accusation.

The glory of Jesus inside of you is like an explosion of light. The light and power of the Living God are present. Just receive it in the places you need it. Let His light bathe you again: soothing, healing, and transforming. He is annihilating those lies, dissolving those wounds, and delivering you with His transforming power.

My Heart's Response

Jesus, let Your light explode every shadow where the enemy has tucked his lies into my mind and heart. I surrender every bit of deception I have believed which is not in Your heart for me. I give it to You now. I want nothing to do with that old way of thinking. Even the unconscious beliefs that influence my life, I give it all to You.

Thank You, Jesus, that under Your headship, I shine. Under Your headship, I remain. You are the true and bright Morning Star who is shining into every crevice of my being. Nothing is hidden from Your searching gaze.

With laser-beam precision, You are cutting away every lie and realigning me with the revelation of who You are. I surrender every thought, Jesus. Let my mind and heart flow in unison with Your holy truth. The wind of Your Spirit is blowing upon me. The brightness of Your glory is illuminating every cell of my being. I sense a fresh space in the spirit. I receive Your gift of freedom today.

Day 51

The Word Within

Break open your Word within me until revelation-light shines out!
Psalm 119:130 TPT

The Word is like a doorway leading to a room filled with the treasures of God's heart; treasures waiting to be discovered by those who seek to know Him. It is here, as we sit with the Lord and engage with His Word and what He's saying to our hearts, that we truly begin to know Him.

When we focus intently on the riches of entwining with the intentions of His heart, we start to understand His will for our lives and the lives of others. His Word breathes into our once guarded stance and frees us to dive deep into His Presence where we can abide.

Immersing ourselves in God's Word is a simple way of entering into encounter. By going into scripture with a single focus—to know Him—the Holy Spirit reveals the heart of Jesus, who is the Word. As we read with open, tender hearts, the Spirit of truth tutors us.

The light of the Word illuminates our path, and we see where Jesus is leading us so that not one step is out of sync with His. Suddenly, we're walking in the truth, sharing the truth, living in it, and expressing it effortlessly. The Living Word eradicates every shadow of darkness and escorts us into liberation; the freedom to be the authentic, pure expressions of who we already are in Him.

My Heart's Response

Jesus, I come to You, asking You to expose any doctrine or way of thinking that doesn't align with Your truth. I reject every condemning belief that has influenced my view of studying scripture. Right now, You are freeing me from the religious spirit that has tried to steal the joy of exploring and relishing You as the Word. A new love for the Word is reigniting in my heart and I am so thankful!

I want to know You. Every day, as I dive into the scriptures, Your Spirit is guiding me. Lies are being stripped away and my belief system is being reframed by profound truth. All pressure is gone. Your Word has become my delight and I am soaking it in. Now I will live in complete freedom—a glorious, clear understanding of the Living Word that is alive within me.

Day 52

God is Rewiring You

...be inwardly transformed by the Holy Spirit through a total reformation of how you think.
This will empower you to discern God's will as you live a beautiful life,
satisfying and perfect in his eyes.
Romans 12:2 TPT

Because of the way we were raised, many of us don't have the neurological wiring to feel secure in God's love and enjoyment of us. We may accept it but struggle to experience it. Today, the Lord is rewiring you. I sense His delight over the way He's moving in you right now. One encounter with Him can miraculously heal and rewire your neurological pathways.

The Spirit of God is releasing white light into your neurological circuitry. He's healing your capacity for joy, the understanding of who you truly are and how He sees you, how much joy you bring to His heart as you are together. All wrong thought patterns are being restructured.

The Lord is healing your sensory capacity in the spirit so that you can experience Him more fully. Your emotional capacity for connection is also being healed. He's removing everything that has hindered your ability to experience your oneness with Him. All pain and trauma sitting at the gate of your access to Him are being demolished.

Tap into the grace that is available to you today. Receive the experience of Jesus moving through you as He rewires your neurological circuitry. God wants you to enjoy the riches of your life with Him and in Him. The Holy Spirit is moving in you, activating this healing deep within. He will make sure that nothing restricts your ability to experience the reality of God in your life.

My Heart's Response

Lord, thank You that I don't have to live in the past. I don't have to consciously or unconsciously rehearse a story about our relationship that You didn't write. Today, I believe You are healing me and reprogramming all thought patterns that aren't in accordance with Your truth. You have given me the mind of Christ so that I can think as You do.

This experience of deep emotional healing is imparting a new understanding of Your love for me. I am receiving an increased ability to enjoy You and our unbreakable bond. Instead of seeing life through the pain of my past, I see it through the lens of Your lavish love. You chose me and want me to experience the certainty of Your love and acceptance. I don't have to pretend anymore! I am loved, and because that truth is sinking in, I will pour out that love without fear.

Day 53

Safe and Secure

And the God of peace will swiftly pound Satan to a pulp under your feet! And the wonderful favor of our Lord Jesus will surround you.

Romans 16:20 TPT

We are holy ground and the Lord is more protective of us than we realize. He is fully invested in us. Nothing is more exhilarating or transforming to the human heart than to know that we are the source of God's joy. We have captured His heart. We are His beloved and He is ours. The beauty of this truth will graciously unfold and expand before us forever.

The enemy's tactics become irrelevant when we live in the wonder and certainty of this divine romance. When we abide in Jesus, the enemy may roar his head off but we remain at peace, safe in the Presence of our King. Keep your eyes fixed on Jesus when hell itself fights for your attention.

Stay connected to the heart of your Protector, Father, Counselor, Redeemer, and King. Jesus is the Lover of your soul. The Father is the source of love, and when you live with your entire being drenched in His love, all fear melts away. It vanishes from your life when you abide in Him because fear cannot exist in the same place as perfect love.

The enemy wants you to live in a lower reality that isn't in alignment with truth. But you are called to live from heaven to earth, to know your identity, be seated with Christ, and live from that place of security.

My Heart's Response

Lord, I never want to drift from the reality of our oneness. Thank You for resetting me today and helping me to refocus my gaze so that I only see truth. You haven't left me and You never will. Your glory is radiating inside of me, expanding in the very center of my being. Love has made me whole, freeing me from fear.

Prince of Peace, I will not yield my thoughts to anyone but You. You have crushed satan under my feet and I will walk in the reality of Your power in me. I am stepping into peace now, trusting the strength of Your perfect love. I will live in the awareness of Your Presence, my mind set on the things of heaven. Above all else, I will guard our connection by slowing down and protecting this gift of peace.

Day 54

The Power of One Encounter

But God now unveils these profound realities to us by the Spirit. Yes, he has revealed to us his inmost heart and deepest mysteries through the Holy Spirit, who constantly explores all things.
1 Corinthians 2:10 TPT

One encounter with Jesus has the power to radically transform your entire life. A single, divine moment changes everything, absolutely everything, about your perception of yourself and God. You may go into His Presence feeling defeated and heavy, but you emerge victoriously. You step in as a pauper and an orphan but come out as a queen or king. Every encounter with God's manifest Presence leaves footprints in your life so that you can look back and remember the truth when you're tempted to forget.

One of the ways you can know that you've had an experience with Jesus is by the changes in your life. Holy encounters leave a mark on your heart; there is unmistakable fruit. Love for God and other people becomes your lifestyle. The Word impacts your heart more deeply. You see things differently. There's more humility and your heart feels like it will explode with gratefulness. Your whole being is reset with truth, and everything immediately lines up to manifest that truth.

Encounters with the Lord draw us closer to Him. They are gifts of glory for us to cherish. Let's honor these revelations with a grateful heart by journaling them, asking Holy Spirit for greater insight, and by sharing them as the Lord leads.

My Heart's Response

Jesus, what an incredible privilege it is to look upon the face of the One in whose image I've been made. Every encounter is precious and life-changing. I'm so grateful, so overcome by Your mercy and grace. I am absolutely lovesick, overwhelmed by the beauty of Your holiness. Through every experience of You, I understand more about who I am as Your bride. Thank You for unveiling my eyes and heart so that I may see and hear You more clearly.

As I stand daily in the Presence of the King, I will soak in the revelations, wisdom, and truths You share. I will honor everything You unveil to my heart by meditating on these precious truths. Thank You for sharing Your secrets, revealing wisdom, and for the images that pour across my vision with beautiful redemption. It is my greatest joy to live with an open heart before You and to be transformed by Your love.

Day 55

Living Gateways

A Prophetic Word

So wake up, you living gateways!
Lift up your heads, you doorways of eternity!
Welcome the King of Glory,
for he is about to come through you.
Psalm 24:7 TPT

Every encounter that I share is your inheritance as well. The revelations are for all of us, so grab these truths and absorb them into your heart.

Several years ago, Jesus took me into heaven. I was pulled through a vortex and found myself standing alongside Jesus. I was completely clothed in sparkling glory—a garment of white light. I had no connection or conscious awareness of the earthly realm. I was fully there, every fiber of my being complete in Christ, filled with the fullness of God. I tasted the age to come and the complete transfiguration of the bride. I stood there as who we are alongside our King, as the counterpart of God.

This is who we are and who we're becoming. As we yield to the Lord and prioritize worshipping the King, He is bringing forth His shining ones—His radiant bride. We are the living gateways He will pour through. As we abide in Jesus, engage Him continuously, and open our spirits wide to Him, God's glory-light will drive out darkness.

This is all that matters now—allowing Him to consume us and loving God with all our heart, mind, and strength. We must live aligned with Him, consumed with God like never before. So, lift up your heads, you doorways of eternity! Welcome the King of Glory, for He is about to come through you.

My Heart's Response

Jesus, I want this. I lift my head as a gateway to the earthly realm and welcome You to consume me, to transfigure me, to be revealed through me. I lay down. I yield to You, Jesus. Thank You that by Your grace, I am growing in stature and strength, in the power of who You are. May my entire being be interwoven with Your perfection, until every part of me aligns with who I am as a new creation in You.

Take the structures of my life as Your wineskin. Remove every blockage so You may pour through the gate of my spirit, unhindered. Jesus, You are my King and the gatekeeper of my life. By Your grace, I am perfectly aligned under Your headship. Welcome, King of Glory, shine through me.

Day 56

His Presence is Home

Jesus replied, "Loving me empowers you to obey my word. And my Father will love you so deeply that we will come to you and make you our dwelling place."

John 14:23 TPT

In the center of our being, where the Lord is, is home. In a vision, I saw multiple doors around our hearts, wide open, and I knew the Lord was telling me that we had left home. We had turned toward distraction and pressure, and stepped out of our safe place, our place of peace, provision, and joy.

In this encounter, we responded by calling every part of our hearts back home. As we did that and sat with Jesus in the center of ourselves again, the peripheral doors closed. The access points that the enemy used to bombard us with fear, anxiety, and a host of other turmoil, were closed. An overwhelming feeling of safety and total relaxation flooded us, and all of the stress completely dissolved.

The Presence of the Lord is our safe place, our home. It is where we're refreshed and find stability, as we settle into the awareness of the One who abides within our spirit. The Lord has chosen to live in these vessels of flesh and blood, to clothe Himself with us and make us His home.

We are in Him and He is in us, but we decide where we will set our affections. Dwelling in His Presence is a choice. Every moment, every new situation, offers us a choice between peace and stress. Will we remain with our hearts centered and settled in His, in the safety of His Presence? Or turn to a door that leads us away from home?

My Heart's Response

Jesus, these revelations are a treasure! What a joy it is to know that I don't have to go in and out of peace, that I can live and move and have my being constantly immersed in the reality of who You are inside of me. Thank You for etching this truth deep inside of my spirit today: we are one. We are inseparable, but I must choose where my heart makes its home.

So today, I choose You all over again. I pick You over every temporary distraction. You are my dwelling place. You are where perfect peace defies trials. I choose to keep my heart safe at home in Your Presence, by keeping the doors of my heart open to only You.

Day 57

He is Redeeming Your Situation

God, you're such a safe and powerful place to find refuge!
You're a proven help in time of trouble—
more than enough and always available whenever I need you.
Psalm 46:1 TPT

Whatever suffering, disappointment, or stress you're going through, God's arm is never too short to save. Maybe your hope has been deferred because of unanswered prayer and you're struggling with confusion? Maybe you feel shut down or ashamed of your unbelief? Know this—Jesus loves you and He wants to redeem your situation. He wants His testimony and His goodness to be experienced through the story of your life.

He isn't mad at you. He hasn't turned away from you. He's right there with you—closer than any human can ever be. Christ in you is your hope of glory. His Presence is the strength of your life. Turn into Him. Just gently turn your attention back to the reality of His Spirit inside of you. He wants to meet every single emotional and practical need that you have. All He asks is that you lean back into Him again.

If this describes you today, let go and quietly engage your heart. Worship until you start to feel His Presence, and as soon as you do, breathe Him in. Stay in that moment, savoring His Presence and drinking His love. Sit with Him as He reignites your awareness of His Presence, who you are, and the authority you carry. You can trust His love. Jesus has defeated everything the enemy has meant for evil, and the Lord is working it together for your good.

My Heart's Response

Lord, I'm so grateful for Your encouragement, so touched by Your compassion. When I feel stuck in the muddy middle of heaviness, You come to my rescue and lead me out of the pit. Your faithfulness never ceases to amaze me.

My heart is engaged with Yours, and every part of my life I yield afresh to You. I'm holding nothing back. You are the strength of my life. My ever-present help who lives within me and meets every need in abundance.

As I yield to You and protect our connection, You're perfecting me and teaching me to trust. My heart is engaged with the beauty of Your Presence within me and I'm awakening to the continual awareness of Your love in every circumstance.

Day 58

Standing Before the King

And the king held out the golden scepter toward Esther.
So Esther arose and stood before the king...
Esther 8:4 NKJV

Be blessed by this encounter, where during a time of worship, I suddenly found myself in heaven. As you read my words, I encourage you to step in and receive what Jesus has for you.

I was standing in the back of a massive throne room in heaven. At the head of the room, Jesus was sitting on His throne. Lining the right side of the room was a company of 'Esthers'—people who, by the Lord's grace, had lived with eyes only for their King. They had lived in beautiful intimacy with Jesus. These 'Esthers' knew the power of their romance with the King. It was their protection, just as it had been for Queen Esther in the Bible.

In the biblical account, Haman sought to kill the Jewish people, including Esther. But because of Esther's intimate relationship and favor with the king, she exposed Haman's plans and the king immediately overturned them. Love for his queen thwarted the enemy's plans. And so it is for us today.

We are invited to live like Esther—completely devoted to Jesus, our King, to join the company of 'Esthers', and to trust the favor extended to us as we walk in holy intimacy with Him. When we prioritize our connection with Jesus, we confidently stand in the Presence of our enemy, knowing our King will demolish the enemy's plans. With our hearts entwined with His, the King extends His scepter of favor and says, "Whatever you want, my love. Whatever you want." Absolute devotion to the Lord is our greatest protection.

My Heart's Response

Jesus, I come before You like Esther, choosing this day to live by Your grace as one wholly devoted, living for the pleasure of my King. Thank You for the favor You have surrounded me with. I'm so grateful that You have enclosed me with angelic protection and wrapped me in Your Presence so that every plan of the enemy against my life comes to nothing.

With my whole heart, I desire to bless You with pure adoration, to move Your heart, and give You joy. Wash me in the oils of cleansing love and wipe away everything that doesn't reflect the beauty of my King. My life is fully yielded to You. I will be the partner You have longed for, standing beside You in the authority You have entrusted me with. Jesus, I desire to see this company of 'Esthers' expand worldwide so that You will receive the reward of Your suffering love.

Day 59

Rest With Him Awhile

But in the depths of my heart I truly know
that you, Yahweh, have become my Shield;
You take me and surround me with yourself.
Your glory covers me continually.
You lift high my head.
Psalm 3:3 TPT

The most traumatic experiences can be overridden by more powerful encounters of God's transforming love. This is what happened in my very first encounter with Jesus. I knew nothing about Him before this. I was clinically depressed and barely surviving. In a sovereign, divine moment, Jesus physically stood in front of me. He looked at me, waves of light pouring from His eyes, a beautiful, iridescent glow radiating from His skin. Pure, healing love poured into me wave after wave.

Love, the most tremendous force of all, saturated me, bringing me back to life. The energy of who God is, bathed every part of me in peace. My coping mechanisms melted. The walls I'd built to survive crumbled in His glory. Every painful memory completely dissolved in a moment, as Love poured Himself into me. Then He reached out His hands and said, "Come with Me. Always come and rest with Me awhile." He led me up a hill where we sat down together, and for a long time, I wept as Jesus' love continued to pour in and completely make me whole.

You can receive everything that Jesus has given me. Enter into this and make it your own. Open your heart to Jesus. See His eyes filled with overflowing love. He is with you and in you. Let go, and be in this moment with Him. Breathe in His Presence and breathe out the stress. Sink into Him as every bit of tension melts away and the powerful experience of His transforming love becomes more significant than all the traumas combined. Come and rest with Him awhile.

My Heart's Response

Jesus, thank You for inviting me to encounter You this way. You care about what I've gone through, and I finally realize that my past isn't more powerful than You are. I don't have to strive to feel You. I don't even need to pray the perfect prayer. I only need to trust Your love and surrender to it. You are my Father, my Daddy, my Savior, Creator, Healer, and Friend; the faithful One who rushes to my side when I've come to the end of myself.

So, I turn my affection to You—back to the reality of Your Spirit within me, and I breathe the atmosphere of Your love. You are encountering me, even now. Even if I haven't experienced Your love in a long, long time. Your love has transformed others, and Your faithful love is doing the same for me. You are here right now, as I rest with You awhile.

Day 60

Remember Who You Are

A Prophetic Word

Rise up in splendor and be radiant, for your light has dawned, and Yahweh's glory now streams from you!
Isaiah 60:1 TPT

As I cast prophetic vision, pull it into your heart. See it. Jesus is the door, so step through Him to embrace everything heaven has for you. This is reality, so engage with it and make it personal so that you can live here. As truth becomes substance in you, heaven and earth unite, and the fullness of Jesus' intentions come to pass.

You are destined to be an inspiration. You are called to be salt and light. It is your destiny to shine as a new creation. You are meant to be a beacon of hope. Before the foundation of the world, God knew you; now, you carry a unique deposit of His nature that no one else has. Though at times you've felt misunderstood, insignificant, and misaligned, the Lord says to lift your eyes to Him. See yourself reflected there and remember who you really are.

Your unique attributes are a gift, a beautiful, one-of-a-kind expression of God that others need to experience. Lift your head! Open your heart! Look at Jesus. See the face of God. The brilliance and radiance you behold are part of you now. His goodness and glory have been deposited in you. What you've experienced up to this point is only a foretaste. Sink deeper into Him and let these truths awaken you.

My Heart's Response

Jesus, Your beauty overwhelms me! To think that I am created in Your image and carry Your glory is astounding. I really am a new creation. I'm not even human anymore! I am a vessel of the most-glorious One. Thank You for this life that You died for me to have. Thank You for inviting me into this love union with Father, Son, and Holy Spirit, for empowering me and shining through me. Thank You for transforming me.

I am beautiful and powerful because of the magnificent One who lives inside of me. I embrace You, Lord! I'm not going to limit myself by what I see in the natural. I'm going to live from a realm of existence that takes me from glory to glory. I will walk in agreement with these truths until every thought submits to Your supreme headship.

Day 61

The Power of Intimacy and Awe

The revelation-light of his Word makes my spirit shine radiant.
Psalm 19:8 TPT

The Word is an access point into the Presence of God. Studying His sovereignty comforts our hearts and obliterates fear. When we sit and ponder the beauty of who Jesus is, intimacy develops. It rekindles our love for Him and increases our capacity to trust and lean on Him. When we meditate on Christ in us, engaging with that reality, studying the awesomeness of the One within us, it floods our mind and heart and realigns us.

Meditating on the profound truths of scripture reignites strength and power in us, but more than that, we lose ourselves. When we gaze on the Word and go into Him, we become more aware of Him than the situations around us. We get caught up in the experience of God in the center of us.

Pondering the sovereignty of God empowers us and protects our hearts. It comforts, exhilarates, and increases our humility as we stand in awe of Him. He is a holy God. When we truly get a glimpse of His sovereignty, it's purifying. The spirit of the fear of the Lord impacts us, and our thoughts, beliefs, words, and actions reflect His worthiness. This holy awe balances intimacy. Intimacy and the awe of God must go together. We're able to receive and then walk in power to express Him with a heart of purity.

My Heart's Response

Lord, I am overwhelmed with the beauty of intimacy and wonder of Your sovereignty. Thank You for choosing me, for filling me with Your Spirit, and entrusting me with something so holy. Your Word has awakened me and changed the very fabric of my being. Your Spirit and Word are my mentors. It seems impossible to truly express my gratitude.

Jesus, You are the Living Word that has pierced my heart and cut away the lies. Your words have brought me back to life, and their power has changed my entire perspective. I will honor the truths and revelations You've given me, for each one is alive.

Holy Spirit, I'm falling in love with You all over again. Jesus, I desire You above all other things. My heart is open to You. My soul is bowed before the beauty of Your majesty. My life will be an exhibit of Your transforming love.

Day 62

Step In

...Held captive by your love, I am truly overcome!
For your undying devotion to me is the most yielded sacrifice.
Song of Songs 6:5 TPT

There's an invitation to a level of intimacy with Jesus right now that's unprecedented. You are being prepared. As you set yourself apart for Him, He brings you forth as a mature, radiant bride. Jesus sees your desire and the Holy Spirit is responding by doing a deep work in you. He knows that you want to live with an undistracted heart, and it thrills Him.

Your heart is being reset so that you can live as you've longed to—so in love with Him, so consumed by Him, so in tune with Him, that everything else grows dim. All of this manifests because your heart and His are flowing with the same desire—that you live in the awareness of holy union.

No longer will you carry a mental posture of separation from the Lord. This gap that inserts itself between your encounters with Him and your emotional day-to-day experience is a delusion that's being dealt with. There is no space between you and God. You and He are one. The grace to live in this revelation is being released to you, and your understanding is being flooded with light.

Your passionate heart has caught His attention. You've leaned in, surrendered, and longed to know Him more, and He has responded. You are rising now into a more complete understanding and expression of who you are as the bride. You are stepping into an entirely different dimension of living.

My Heart's Response

Jesus, I sense myself becoming steadier in my walk. Humble confidence in our union is literally transforming me. The abiding awareness of Your Presence is reframing my thinking. Thank You for the way You've been changing me. I feel it. The sense of separation is diminishing, and I am becoming immovable in our position together.

Everything about my life is being consumed with this heavenly reality. You are with me, continually drawing me closer even when I get distracted. Your grace met me and is flooding me with revelation light. I'm standing in a deluge of glory now, every single moment. Even when I'm faced with difficulties, I sense Your Presence with me. I am becoming immovable in my faith—a pillar in the house of my God.

Day 63

A Brand New Day

But we all, with unveiled face, beholding as in a mirror the glory of the Lord, are being transformed into the same image from glory to glory, just as by the Spirit of the Lord.

2 Corinthians 3:18 NKJV

The great unveiling of Christ is dawning in your heart. Truth is blasting into you with strength and power. Can you tell that you're different? Because you are. His love is literally transforming you in every way. You have been awakened with God's divine kiss. The Living Word has come in power to settle you and clear your vision.

Revelation is pouring into you, and everything about the way you think is being completely overhauled. Those limitations of the past that once strangled your faith no longer exist. Now you are rising from strength to strength in the Presence of the King. It's time for you to soar.

The experience of Jesus residing inside of you is becoming a reality. As you lean into Him, the stresses that once plagued you are becoming less evident. Your emotions are coming in line, and you're beginning to experience wholeness in every area of your spirit, soul, and body.

As you spend time beholding Jesus, His tangible Presence is dissolving the obscurities that have limited your capacity to believe and flow with

Him. Your faith is growing. Grab ahold of this encouragement today. Take it to heart, make it personal, and never let it go, and you will notice greater freedom, security, and faith. This is a brand new day!

My Heart's Response

Jesus, thank You for unveiling my heart to see You more clearly. You're peeling back the doubt that left a muddy film on my soul. Today, a fresh breath of encouragement has awakened faith inside of me. Truth is washing my soul, changing me in ways that I never knew were possible. I don't have to live distracted by the past. Stress does not need to be a normal part of my life. You created me for so much more!

Every morning I will turn my eyes to You and bathe You with my love. I will spend my waking hours walking in the awe and wonder of You inside of me. You will hold my awareness. I will honor the holiness that has made its home in my heart. And if I become distracted, if I momentarily get tangled in a web of disillusionment, I will return my gaze to You. I will sit under the water spout of Your love until every part of me is glimmering with the essence of Your beauty.

Day 64

Empowered by Love

Behold, how good and pleasant it is
when brothers dwell in unity.
...For there the Lord has commanded the blessing,
life forevermore.
Psalm 133:1, 3 ESV

Love, the greatest force of all, has come. When you accepted this holiest gift, you were sealed and set apart. No power in the entire world can separate you from Him now. His love has set you free. The very fabric of your being has been imprinted with the Father's DNA. Your identity and His are the same. You don't need to wait to feel the effects of these wonders to accept them. This is authentic, pure, holy truth. Nothing is greater than the Person of love inside of you. And love is meant to be shared.

This radical transformation in us is meant to shine like a city on a hill. It's meant to radiate God's heart by showing the world what love, compassion, and unity look like. It is in the place of unity that God's commanded blessing is released; blessing that transforms cultures.

When we are personally fulfilled and consumed in the experience of Jesus' love, it flows easily from us. We see value in every person we encounter. We look for ways to encourage and empower when we're healed from fear-driven self-protection. When love has set us free, our primary concern is releasing that love everywhere we go. Unity creates an uninterrupted flow of the Spirit of God that spreads around the globe. Love changes everything.

My Heart's Response

Lord, thank You for awakening me to the power of love that You've entrusted to me. The reality of Your love has flowed into my heart like healing oil, and I desire to share it with others. Criticism and backbiting will not be a part of my atmosphere. Fear of rejection will not hold me back. I have been empowered by love!

Now, my perspective has changed. I see others through the filter of Your heart. I am beginning to experience the continuous flow of Your Spirit working to unite Your beautiful bride. How glorious it is that we're becoming aware of who we are so that we shine into the darkness!

For me, I will stay tuned in to Your heart so that the purity of love backs every single word, action, and motive. I will do my part to live as You've called me to live, to delight Your heart by empowering others with love.

Day 65

Creating With Him

A Prophetic Word

"Prophesy over these bones, and say to them..."
So I prophesied as I was commanded. And as I prophesied, there was a sound,
and behold, a rattling, and the bones came together, bone to its bone.
Then he said to me, "Prophesy to the breath; prophesy, son of man, and say to the breath, Thus
says the Lord God: Come from the four winds, O breath, and breathe on these slain, that they may live."
Ezekiel 37:4, 7, 9 ESV

God wants to create through us and touch planet earth like never before. He is giving us a heart of creativity in ways we've never dreamed. This call is more brilliant than we could have imagined. It not only flows from artists, singers, dancers, writers, and musicians; it is a living substance of life pouring through us. We are the paintbrushes held in the Master's hand, co-creating a magnificent future!

The Lord says, "The future is ours to create from this moment. We will use a color palette of compassion, kindness, and authentic love. My Spirit will move through you, flooding you with the full spectrum of true light. The future is union, oneness, living within Me, reigning together in the restoration of all things, and bringing forth My Kingdom."

God is breaking us free from restricting mindsets and attitudes of the heart. With a Kingdom mindset, we will paint with kindness, healing, wisdom, and compassion. Breathtaking beauty will arise from the ashes, and all things will be made new. We will release a sound that breaks the earth's frustration and heals humanity. Everything will respond to the sound as He speaks and creates through us!

My Heart's Response

Lord, I want to walk in the profoundness of this word. Thank You for the incredible privilege of creating with You! My natural mind cannot grasp the power and authority You have entrusted to me, so instead, I will embrace it with my heart. I will trust the truth that we are one. I don't have to understand to believe. I simply need to sit in the awe and wonder as they escort me to You.

I believe I will see Your beauty moving through my hands, words, and actions. As I live in tune with the harmony of heaven, I will speak Your words and release Your heart. Together, we will paint the earth with compassion, kindness, and healing, until every soul recognizes Your brushstrokes of love.

Day 66

Ruling From Rest

For those of us who believe, faith activates the promise and we experience the realm of confident rest!
Hebrews 4:3 TPT

I want to share a truth that will shift you. In a holy encounter, I stood inside of Jesus as the corporate bride. His right arm of authority moved slowly through the air in front of Him. This sweeping motion, done in supreme authority, moved a dark energy that was before Him. It was effortless and absolute.

The two things that stood out to me were that He cleared the air effortlessly and that His arm and ours were one. Jesus, the King who has all authority, is reminding us of our position in Him. We will shift spiritual environments with ease when we believe that we are in Christ, clothed with His divinity, and seated with Him in heavenly places. But before we can alter the atmosphere around us, we must change our own.

We mustn't allow negative energy to become normal. Any feeling of uneasiness, dissonance, anxiety, or heaviness coming from the demonic realm must not be tolerated. Jesus wants us to recognize the power we have in Him. He wants us to rule and reign with Him in confidence, humility, and a secure heart.

We are royalty, and He's pulling us into position so that anything in our lives not authored by Jesus will be removed—effortlessly swept away. We stand in our most significant authority when we see ourselves as He sees us—not as victims, but as His bride who rules from a place of rest.

My Heart's Response

Jesus, I set my heart in obedience. You are the only legitimate influence that I will receive in my life. Thank You for lifting me into a new mindset and teaching me to align myself with Your wisdom. Your ways are higher than mine, so much easier and simpler than I once expected. I'm amazed at how effortless it is to live in victory. I only need to believe in Your love for me.

I am who You say I am. I am Your anointed bride who rules and reigns with You. So, I pray for Your beautiful, corporate bride to rise to her throne of responsibility, to stand saturated and radiant with Your Presence. I pray we will accept the power of the finished work of the Cross and shine with Your heart. Thank You for this privilege. Thank You for awakening us to the truth that we can govern with You in this realm and bring heaven to earth.

Day 67

God of Abundance

And God is able to make all grace [every favor and earthly blessing] come in abundance to you, so that you may always [under all circumstances, regardless of the need] have complete sufficiency in everything [being completely self-sufficient in Him], and have an abundance for every good work and act of charity.
2 Corinthians 9:8 AMP

The Lord is pulling lack off of you right now. Whatever's lacking in your life—finances, faith, family, relationships, or confidence, the God of abundance is replenishing your resources. He's removing lack-mindedness, poverty mindsets, and orphan spirits. Love is annihilating every fear that has plagued you, whether it's the fear of man, of being alone, of rejection, or any other lie. Instead, you'll manifest abundance.

Christ's sufficiency overrules every insufficiency in your life. He brings not only a financial blessing but a wealth of prosperity in every area. Fruitfulness blossoms from the One who is a tree of life within you. His wisdom, knowledge, and the abundance of His nature permeate you. It seeps into your circumstances, relationships, and the way you view setbacks. It releases strength in the areas where fear tries to take you out.

In the encounter I shared yesterday, where Jesus' hand repelled the intention of darkness, it also did something else. When the Lord's arm moved over the same space again, glory was released. The recreative, supernatural Presence and peace of God bathed everything in its path. His provision filled the space where the darkness was. He filled the void with Himself. He impregnated it with the beauty of who He is. The emptiness became saturated with abundance. This is what He is doing in your life today.

My Heart's Response

Jesus, I say *yes* to this incredible promise! Thank You for demolishing lack, and flooding my dry ground with life to produce fruit in every area. Your provision for me is complete, and nothing is missing. You are my sufficiency. I can sense peace where previously I only felt the void of emptiness and lack.

You are with me and strengthening me. You are filling me with Yourself. The shalom of God is my portion. Wholeness and provision are Your desires for me, and I receive them. In You, every promise has found its *amen*. In Your Presence is fullness of joy, and I feel it rising in my spirit. You are the fulfillment of my life. You are the great I AM, the God of abundance. Today, I step into the freedom to enjoy my life with You.

Day 68

Letting Love Lead Us

This is My commandment, that you love and unselfishly seek the best for one another, just as I have loved you. No one has greater love [nor stronger commitment] than to lay down his own life for his friends.
John 15:12-13 AMP

We are the lovesick bride who has been healed by Jesus' perfect love. And now, we are called to share that love. One way to do this is by making it our passion to speak life and encouragement to the people in our lives.

We demonstrate a Kingdom culture by valuing and truly engaging every single person we interact with. Let's make them feel seen, heard, and important. Let's give people a taste of God's love by giving them our full attention while gently leaning into the Lord as He guides the conversation. When we allow ourselves to be present with others—listening, encouraging, consoling, asking questions, and truly enjoying them, it becomes a source of healing and empowerment to them.

Genuinely connecting with others on a heart level is a source of massive healing. I encourage you to be mindful of this. The Lord longs for us to build each other up in our most holy faith, to show compassion, and to champion each other.

It isn't enough to experience His love and hide it for ourselves. Love is meant to be shared. It's so beautiful to have this mindset as a core value because it truly manifests Jesus to the world. Let's be this example of Jesus. Let's receive and value others the way we want to be received. Let's let love lead us in all we do and say.

My Heart's Response

Thank You, Jesus, for shifting our culture and shifting my heart. I will be a reflection of Your heart to every single person I meet. Holy Spirit, flow into every word and conversation so that everyone I encounter is touched with Your life, power, and healing. I will lean into You and You will guide my words, attitudes, and the posture of my heart.

Lord, I want to be remembered for my love. So I will do my part to make others feel valued and important, the same way You make me feel. You have radically transformed my life and healed me in ways I never dreamed possible. Now, I want to be that life and light to others. I want to be a blessing to every person You entrust to me.

Day 69

Empowered to Believe

My old identity has been co-crucified with Christ and no longer lives. And now the essence of this new life is no longer mine, for the Anointed One lives his life through me—we live in union as one!
Galatians 2:20 TPT

In difficult times, when you're barely hanging on and have no capacity to believe, this scripture will be life to you. This verse tells us that we don't get breakthroughs by gritting our teeth and trying to force faith into operation. It's the opposite. When we fully let go of every concern and pressure, releasing the totality of our lives into the Lord's hands, Jesus takes over. His victory becomes ours. The Anointed One, alive inside of us, empowers us to believe.

When we stop depending on ourselves to manifest peace, patience, and faith, Jesus graciously breathes them into us. All He asks is that we sink back into Him. The Spirit of God coursing through you, awakens you to a reality that stands in blatant contradiction to the chaos around you. Christ in you is the hope of glory and the surety of everything you've believed for. He is our reality.

You don't have to live the Christian life in your strength. That's not the Gospel. The Lord wants every single moment of every day to be a supernatural experience, where His life dispenses through us, infusing us with strength, faith, and hope that we can't manifest on our own.

My Heart's Response

Jesus, I turn the attention of my heart back to You. I shift out of stress, into the awareness of Your divine nature inside of me. You are the Prince of Peace who calms the raging storms. Take over, Lord. I'm done struggling to make things happen. I'm done trying to understand without Your perspective. I can't fix everything! But I can surrender afresh.

Lord, thank You for giving me the strength to continue when I don't have strength of my own. Your Spirit in me is my life now. It gives substance to an entirely new way of existence. Because of You, I have a supernatural capacity to live in the peace that defies every trial. You're giving me a fresh grace to believe. I'm resting now in the truth that You have everything under control. I don't want to do it on my own, and I don't have to. In You, I have everything I need.

Day 70

The Master Potter

A Prophetic Word

But now, O Lord
You are our Father
We are the clay, and You our potter
And all we are the work of Your hand.
Isaiah 64:8 NKJV

Jesus is doing a work of restoration and healing in you. The gentleness, majesty, and tender loving care of the Lord are reaching out to you today. Our Shepherd, the majestic King of Glory, is dealing with issues in your life because it is time for you to rise to an inexplicable degree of freedom, unlike anything you've ever experienced before.

The Master Potter, the Creator, the Lover of your soul, is massaging the clay of your heart. He is molding and smoothing out every crack and breakage. Where the demonic has attacked you and life has taken its toll, Jesus is gently breathing His Spirit into you.

Lean into Him right now, as He works His thumbs ever so gently into your heart, like a tender kiss. Jesus is gently pouring water on the clay of your heart, softening it like clay on a wheel, as He smooths, molds, fills in every crack, and perfects every aspect. It doesn't matter how deep that crack or break is; Jesus the Healer is bringing you forth perfected. The Master Potter's touch is making all things new.

Keep your attention, the eyes of your heart, fixed on the face of Jesus. Settle into His arms as He takes you deeper now. His life-giving touch is taking you from glory to glory. Engage with this by faith and receive the shift. This heart surgery is transforming you now.

My Heart's Response

Jesus, I adore You. You are my life, my very breath. Thank You for this amazing invitation and promise. I feel Your gentle hands working out every kink, massaging my heart with the oily substance of love that is causing trauma and pain to fall away easily. I feel Your love pouring into my being—perfect love that drives out fear. You are healing me and shaping me into Your image so that I bear Your likeness with no cracks in my soul.

I am secure in You, safely wrapped in Your arms that held me before time began. I receive this miraculous work of healing and freedom. My soul is coming into perfect alignment with Your Spirit. I am a holy vessel, fit for my King. You have made me whole, and nothing—no fear, disappointment, or strategy of the enemy will ever separate me from You. Lover of my soul, You have washed me in healing blood, and I am free.

Day 71

Reservoirs of Wisdom

Since we first heard about you, we've kept you always in our prayers that you would receive the perfect knowledge of God's pleasure over your lives, making you reservoirs of every kind of wisdom and spiritual understanding.

Colossians 1:9 TPT

In the above verse, Paul prayed the heart of the Father for us—that we would receive the perfect knowledge of God's pleasure over our lives. The word 'knowledge' can also be translated, 'the experience of'. In essence, Paul prayed that every part of our hearts would experience the absolute joy and pleasure that we bring the Lord just by being ourselves.

Do you feel your heart rising in anticipation as you read that? We are all desperate for more of this reality, and the good news is that Jesus longs for the same. He wants us to live in the experience of the Gospel—the reality of His life inside of us.

That's why the enemy fights so hard against the experiential Gospel; he doesn't want us to live in the certainty of our union with Christ because then we'll become an unstoppable force. But Jesus wants us to wrap our hearts with this truth so that it floods us with wisdom, confidence, and the knowledge of who He is.

These spiritual truths make us come alive! They pierce the deepest parts of our soul with life and joy that go much deeper than our natural understanding. Let's connect with Paul's prayer and invite Jesus to illuminate our hearts with the knowledge of God's pleasure over us.

My Heart's Response

Lord, Your desire is coming across loud and clear. You love me more extravagantly than my limited understanding can grasp. You long for me to experience the power of our holy union. By faith, I enter into a more profound experience of this divine romance, of our oneness, of Your unfathomable love. I will sit and ponder this beautiful truth with You until it is my everyday reality. You are making it come alive to me!

Thank You for pouring this truth into my heart: You delight in me. In me! My heart is overwhelmed by this truth, but don't stop pouring it in, Lord. Don't stop because it is finally becoming an unshakable truth to my heart. You are ushering me into a deeper experience of this very holy reality. You are taking me from one degree of glory to the next, and I'm coming alive because of this perfect knowledge You've unveiled to my heart.

Day 72

This Is Our Inheritance

For he enjoys his faithful lovers.
He adorns the humble with his beauty,
and he loves to give them victory.
Psalm 149:4 TPT

We have inherited everything that Jesus is—love, holiness, wisdom, peace, royalty, and more because we now live in Christ. Christ in us, the hope (that word means 'absolute, total surety') of glory. It's not future, wishful thinking. It means 'the absolute, total certainty of'. We can step into the consciousness of His Presence at any moment, and become certain of His glory surging through us. As we engage Him, light engulfs our soul. His love becomes more real than anything we go through.

The more we live in this heavenly reality, the more evident our transformation is. We are coming forth as shining ones. When we fully engage with the Lord in us, we begin to live from heaven to earth. We bring His reality into ours. We begin to experience a continual, ecstatic state that actually grounds us in the surety of who we are as sons and daughters of God.

Christ is bringing forth a people who look, sound, and love the way He does, who live from faith in the finished work of the Cross and remain cloaked in Christ. And as we do, we will operate in daily life from inside the Father's heart. This is what Jesus died for us to inherit. This is our birthright.

My Heart's Response

Lord, the more time I spend with You, the more I'm becoming absolutely certain of Your love. It's so powerful! Your love is changing me in every way. I don't think the same way anymore. I don't even feel the same way, physically. Every fiber of my being is completely drenched with love and truth.

You are strengthening me at my very core. You are what centers me. Thank You for demolishing the things that used to squeeze the life out of my soul. Love has made me so radiant that I hardly recognize myself.

And so, I engage You without reservation, so grateful for this inheritance You've given me. I bow before this One whose holiness has made me come alive. Every day as I turn to You, You're perfecting me. You have beautified Your bride with a garment of glory. You have beautified us with Yourself. This is our inheritance.

Day 73

You're Safe Here

There is no fear in love, but perfect love casts out fear. For fear has to do with punishment, and whoever fears has not been perfected in love.
1 John 4:18 ESV

There is no fear in God. God is perfect love. And as we stand inside of Him, inside of perfect love, fear is absent. It simply doesn't exist inside of Him.

On the Cross, Jesus conquered every single opposition to a blessed and overcoming life. He took our infirmity upon Himself. He took every bit of brokenness and bondage. He paid the price for our freedom in every way. Things that trigger us, curses in our bloodlines, demonic strongholds, and hindrances to our intimacy with God—He took the lot and exchanged it for beauty. He exchanged our darkness for light.

Jesus' suffering love has given us life; true life, the way God intended. As we engage Him, turning into the enfolding of His Presence, we receive. We rest and grow in confidence in His love and His faithfulness. As we sit with Him, His glory-light saturates whatever we're dealing with—internal areas of brokenness, external resistance, storms that need collapsing, and everything changes.

He is for you. He loves you. There is a permanent *yes* in His heart for you. This is your moment to receive His promises that you have held in your heart. Stay here, beloved. Stay in His Presence, in the truth, in the light. Let Him make you whole as you choose to believe again. You're safe here, with Jesus.

My Heart's Response

Jesus, I feel Your love gently enveloping me like a warm summer breeze. You know these insecurities that try to lure me away from faith. You see the fears that reach for my heart. But right here, in the security of Your love, I know that I'm safe. Thank You for the price You paid so that I can be free. Thank You for shining glory-light into the darkness so that I can see.

Lord, I won't push away the truth You're offering. I'm not afraid to believe anymore. You are perfect love and Your love for me has become the substance to my faith, the very strength of my life. Your blood declared my freedom. You're right here with me, even when I temporarily get distracted. You're always so kind, so patient. I'm ready now, Lord. Your love has made me strong. I can face anything when I remember You're with me.

Day 74

Remember Who You Are

And this Light never fails to shine through darkness—
Light that darkness could not overcome.
John 1:5 TPT

I've been in heaven and stood as us in the future. I was privileged to witness a tiny taste of who we truly are and are becoming: shining ones who release the brilliance and perfection of God's nature. As we stand in the Presence of the King, we become more and more radiant. Even now, with our hearts turned to Him, the King is drenching us with glory-light. And in this light, darkness cannot remain.

Staying in Him, keeping our focus on Jesus no matter what, causes His light to infiltrate every shadow of darkness. Living from this consistent inner stance, causes us to radiate Jesus into every situation. His Presence escorts us into victory. Warfare becomes more about remaining in Him than it does about fighting.

Overcoming isn't about fighting demons. They've already been defeated on the Cross. It's a lot less complex than we've understood. Victory is obtained when we know the power of the Blood and understand our true nature. Darkness can only be eradicated by light, so we must remain in the light. We draw on the life of who He is, stay in it, and simply release it. We fix our eyes on Jesus because the more we behold Him, the more we understand who we are.

My Heart's Response

Lord, I'm in awe of Your ways. The truths You're infusing into my heart are transforming me. They're so powerful, yet so simple. The more I yield to You, the greater my depth of surrender, the more I feel the stability of Your Spirit in me. Thank You for instructing me and giving me the grace to remain connected to the Source of victory. This is how I will live as an overcomer who shines with Your radiant beauty.

Jesus, I'm drawing from Your nature in me so that I can stand firm. The same Spirit that had the power to raise You from the dead, lives in my mortal body. Faith in this truth collapses the enveloping darkness. The more I get to know You, the easier it is to keep my mind set on the things that are good, holy, and true. And in this place of continual awareness, Your truth comforts me. Light, power, and authority flow through my every word. In this confident and humble place of union, darkness cannot overwhelm me. When I fix my eyes on You, I remember who I am.

Day 75

Freedom From Religion

A Prophetic Word

Having begun by the Spirit, are you now being perfected by the flesh?
Galatians 3:3 ESV

In the spirit, I saw us encircled with a spiral of dark energy made up of words. This swirl of words framed our belief systems and perspective. They became beliefs we live from, causing emotional reactions in us to what we believe. Jesus appeared and pressed His forehead into mine, and I knew He was doing it for all of us. Kindness, gentleness, and absolute sovereignty flowed from Him into me. It was resetting our understanding and untangling us from the spirit of religion.

Jesus said that He was setting us free from the entanglement and impact of the religious spirit and its many facets. Receive this into your heart now. He is breaking control. He is demolishing fear and punishment-based living. Religious striving is falling off of you. Lies that have influenced your life and the understanding of who you are, are being burned away. You are being freed from torment and deception.

Right now, the Spirit of Truth is moving with fresh power through you. Beams of light radiating from Christ inside you are dismantling the negative energy that has encircled you. Demonically energized words, religious spirits, and spirits of control and fear are breaking in your life. Lean into this grace that is pouring from the Lord right now. This is your moment of deliverance.

My Heart's Response

Jesus, I thank You for this shift today. I surrender to You and sink into the power of this moment. I receive Your power radiating within me and freeing me from these spirits of deception, religion, and control. Thank You that the tentacles of fear, intimidation, offense, and manipulation are being severed from my life.

As I lean into You, into this grace, thank You that Your mighty breath is blowing like a hurricane of love, annihilating the swirl of these demonic words. You are shifting me and reframing my belief systems with truth. I align myself now with Your truth. You love me and dispense Your life into mine, flowing Your righteousness through me, freeing me, and empowering me to shine with the virtues of Your own nature.

You are my true life, the power of who I am now. You are the only One I want to reflect, and I will do so by Your grace alone. I relinquish control. I lean back into the arms of Your Presence and trust You as my Shepherd. Thank You for untangling me from the spirit of religion and from every other influence of darkness. Thank You for freeing me today and filling me again with Your Spirit.

Day 76

The Miraculous Work of Love

Who is this coming up from the wilderness,
Leaning upon her beloved?
Song of Solomon 8:5 NKJV

I feel the wooing of the Lord drawing you into His healing, miraculous love. Your situation and everything you're facing may be stressful or seem hopeless, but I can testify that one moment in His arms changes everything. He loved me back to life when I didn't even know it was possible. My situation was still the same; I was in an abusive marriage and my life was a mess, but Jesus healed my soul completely.

Through this experience, I learned the power of His love that strips trauma of its hold. I experienced it so I could tell you that it's real. Jesus will heal your heart when you lean into His. It's okay that you sometimes doubt. He isn't mad at you for that. Like the Shulamite, lean on your Beloved who will lead you out of this wilderness.

Nothing is outside of Jesus' redemptive power. His miraculous work of love is a healing balm for your soul. His perfect love is strong enough to set you free. He loves you beyond words. He's right there. Close your eyes and sink into the arms of grace. He's got you. When all you can do is lean, leaning is enough.

My Heart's Response

Jesus, when I barely have the strength to lift my eyes, I will lift my heart. I'm leaning in full dependence into Your safe embrace. Once and for all, I'm letting these broken pieces of my heart fall through my fingers and into Your healing hands. I'm trusting the miraculous work of love that You have begun.

You haven't forgotten me. You are the door that stands open before me, welcoming me into freedom. And today, I step in. Thank You for rescuing me, for leading me out of this wilderness that felt like it would swallow me whole.

Thank You for Your nearness right now. You haven't abandoned me. You've been here all along. Your perfect peace wraps me and holds me tight. I finally sense the internal noise quieting down. My soul has found its Savior. My heart has found its home. Love has come, and my soul is free!

Day 77

Kalah

When he had sipped the sour wine, he said, "It is finished, my bride!" Then he bowed his head and surrendered his spirit to God.
John 19:30 TPT

On one occasion, Jesus took me to the throne room. There were myriads of people—just thousands upon thousands of worshippers in this huge room, surrounding the throne of grace. Over and over and over, in one accord, they shouted, "It is finished! It is finished! It is finished!"

Their declaration went straight into my spirit and down into the earth. I immediately knew that the revelation of the finished work of the Cross was being added to the body of Christ at this time. The message of the blood of Jesus, what He's done for us, what His blood has given us access to, are going to be center stage.

Jesus' last words on the Cross were, "It is finished." This is the word, 'kalah', which has a homonym that means 'fulfilled [completed]' and 'bride'. With His last breath, Jesus made a declaration of love for us. In essence, He was letting us know that the price for our betrothal had been paid. We can be with Him forever because an eternal covenant has been made.

Connect your heart to heaven's shouts of, "It is finished!" Everything you need has been taken care of at Calvary. As you meditate on the all-encompassing power of the Cross, remember that it is a fulfillment of trustworthy, faithful love. From now on, every need has already been met. It is past tense. Finished. Promised and fulfilled because of His love for the bride.

My Heart's Response

Jesus, Your love is astounding! You took care of my every need before I ever came to the earth. You declared my victory before I ever experienced a trial. Your perfect love took care of everything in advance. It's hard for my natural mind to comprehend such passion and power, but I gratefully accept this perfect gift.

This message of the Cross and the power of Your blood will be my meditation today. I will remember what it cost You to be with me forever. My heart will sing of a love so complete in its redeeming power, it could never be overturned. You thought of everything ahead of time so we would never be separated.

I echo the cries of heaven, "It is finished!" Everything within me is aligning to this experience, and I'm rising as Your beloved bride. Nothing can stand against the power of Your blood. Faith in Your love has freed me.

Day 78

God's Unfailing Love

For if you embrace the truth, it will release true freedom into your lives.

John 8:32 TPT

Today, the Holy Spirit is moving in your midst. As you sit under the waterfall of His cascading love, He is permeating your body and soul with glory. He is crashing into your mind and emotions with truth and healing. Jesus is pouring liquid love into the areas of your heart that have suffered mistreatment, abuse, or been subjected to the horrific, demonically energized behaviors of others. Whatever has happened, no matter how extreme, if parts of your heart feel trapped in time, stuck in the traumas of the past, know this—Jesus is outside of time.

The Alpha and Omega, the Beginning and the End, is moving up and down the timeline of your life, into every area where you've felt stuck. The Spirit of God is flooding every memory and trauma that still holds pain. He is bathing and saturating your heart in glory. Gentleness, love, and peace are drowning painful memories until they no longer dictate your thoughts, reactions, or emotions.

He is in you, integrating glory into every cell, every memory, even into the subconscious memories you've suppressed. He's bringing you forth whole. He is transforming you from the inside out. Receive this fresh infusion. Nothing is too hard for Him, and He is overturning your pain so that it shines as a testimony of His unfailing love.

My Heart's Response

Lord, I feel faith rising in me, and I'm ready for You to reign over every conscious and subconscious thought. Thank You for coming as my Healer and Deliverer today. I believe that Your glory is powerful enough to eradicate traumatic memories. You are here, drowning the noise of pain with Your songs of love.

My entire being is infused with the reality of how absolutely powerful You are. I'm becoming aware of Your abiding Presence that is realigning my thoughts with Yours. Every day, my mind settles into the wonder of holy truth, and that truth is reconfiguring the way I think.

My conscious awareness is being consumed by Your glory within me on a more consistent basis. My heart is flowing with images of Your beauty where shadows of darkness once blocked the view. You're creating new beliefs in my heart and washing me ever so tenderly in the healing flow of love.

Day 79

Hearing and Seeing God

Lovers of God have been given eyes to see
and ears to hear from God.
Proverbs 20:12 TPT

Jesus is unveiling your heart in a greater way and pouring out fresh revelation. He is clearing your spiritual vision and anointing your eyes with eye salve so that you can see Him more clearly. He has heard the cries of your heart to know Him and He is responding. Your spiritual ears will catch the sound of heaven now. Your heart will feel His purifying fire as He whispers secrets and awakens you to the subtle intonations of His voice.

One word from God spoken to your heart, can radically change your entire existence. He is the force behind that word. He is the life and creative power that spoke the Universe into existence. He is the Word! He is the Life! He is the mystery of heaven living inside of you. As you tap into Jesus' Presence, you'll see, hear, and notice the wonders unfolding before you; exploding within you. And as you drink in these mysteries, they will transform you.

Each day, you'll feel your heart stirring, longing to reveal Him everywhere you go. In humility, you'll step into your role as a king, priest, and shining one. You won't be defined by how you feel or who others say you are. You'll be defined by nothing other than who God says you are because knowing Him defines your very existence.

My Heart's Response

Jesus, I say *yes* to Your invitation, *yes* to the eye salve. You are clearing my spiritual vision and opening my ears. Thank You for unveiling my heart so that I may know You like never before. I'm embracing the mystery, Lord. I want to be changed so profoundly that I scarcely recognize myself.

My heart is flowing with one main theme—to know You. Everything about my life now centers around this desire. You are my breath, my hope, the substance of my very existence. Your Word is alive inside of me, piercing into the marrow of my bones, becoming a part of me.

As I see You more clearly, all other distractions are beginning to fade. You're directing my thoughts and dreams. I'm looking You in the eyes, and You are leading me by Your tender gaze. Each day is becoming an adventure that I anticipate because I know that You are here.

Day 80

You Are Radiant

A Prophetic Word

And standing beside you, glistening in your pure and golden glory, is the beautiful bride-to-be!
Psalm 45:9 TPT

In a vision, I experienced us as the bride. I was walking, dressed, and filled with the virtue and nature of Jesus radiating from me in gleaming light. I was walking at an incline, ascending. My walk was steady and stable because the gaze of my heart was locked onto Jesus. Nothing was able to distract me from Him. I was motivated by an absolute adoration for who He is. I could not be moved from the priority of my relationship with Him and the certainty of who I am in Him. I knew that all else flowed from this posture of heart.

As I walked toward Jesus, I saw that He was not just One seated on the throne, but He was the throne. Jesus is the seat of all authority. He turned to watch me take my place alongside Him. Multitudes of angels and people in heaven were celebrating with massive rejoicing because we, in this dispensation of time, had fully awakened to the truth of who we are and the absolute authority we carry.

We were focused, immovable, and utterly free, taking our rightful position alongside our King as His royal bride. I could feel their love for us and their excitement for what was happening. This is the experience the Holy Spirit is bringing us into.

He is calling for the bride to make herself ready. By fixing our heart's gaze on our King, we will be immovable, steady in our walk, unencumbered by religion, and undistracted by the cares of this world, so that we can take our place beside Him and enter into this unprecedented time of co-reigning to bring the Kingdom on earth.

My Heart's Response

Lord, let this be the posture of my heart, always. With my eyes locked on Yours, my gaze completely consumed with only You, and my life unreservedly surrendered to You, I will rise in power and authority. Thank You for glorifying me with Yourself, for strengthening me in Your Presence.

My soul is bowed before You. I am undone, humbled by the incomprehensible honor I have to stand alongside the most-glorious, magnificent King. I receive Your grace to live this way, always—focused, stable, and immovable, so my life will glorify You, and the meditation of my heart will rise as a sweet fragrance. I make myself ready for You, Beautiful One. My life radiates with Your glory.

Day 81

You Are Perfect

Therefore you shall be perfect, just as your Father in heaven is perfect.
Matthew 5:48 NKJV

The Lord is sharing His heart with us. He has chosen to unveil Himself completely, to reveal mysteries and open the scriptures to us with fresh insight. He is drawing us closer than we've ever been. What a humbling honor it is to be trusted with the heart of God.

The very core of our heart is coming into agreement with the full power and pure intention of God's love. When we know Him in this intimate way, we become consumed with the beauty and security of who He is. We find ourselves utterly liberated and free in the center of our being. We become obsessed with fulfilling His desires because we're wrecked by the truth that He chose us to carry His heart. Us! Frail, insignificant ones who have become vessels of purity, majesty, and perfection.

Religion teaches that we can only attain a tiny level of perfection through what becomes exhausting self-effort. We end up trapped in shame, feeling unworthy of God's promises. But Jesus reconnects us to the truth of our identity. We are worthy of housing the most-glorious One because of what He did. All we're required to do is surrender and believe that we no longer live, but Christ lives in us (see Galatians

2:20). We are moving into the truth of who we are as new creations, to live from the strength of our union with Christ; one heart, one nature, so that we can release the truth of who Jesus is to the world.

My Heart's Response

Lord, I'm in awe that I have always been in Your heart. When all I saw was a pitiful mess, You saw me perfected. You saw me in the future and brought it into the now. Thank You that I am complete in You. I am whole because of You. You have entrusted me to carry the treasure of Your heart, the most glorious and precious gift of glory, so I can share You with others.

You have become my obsession, my breath, and my only view of life. Your divine nature has consumed every ounce of my imperfection; it simply doesn't exist anymore because the Perfect One has become my life. You have become one with me, and now we live in a union so holy, it's hard for me to grasp. All that You are, I am. My heart is finally connecting to the reality of this miraculous truth.

Day 82

Welcome Home

Deep within me are these lovesick longings, desires and daydreams of living in union with you. When I'm near you, my heart and my soul will sing and worship with my joyful songs of you, my true source and spring of life!

Psalm 84:2 TPT

You have been delivered from the kingdom of darkness and escorted into the Kingdom of light. Welcome home! The realm of His Presence is home forever. The glory of God in your interior life is where you come alive as you rest in Him. Truly alive! With every unfolding revelation, each time Jesus lifts the veil a little bit more, transformation takes place. This is your life now. You have found the One your soul loves, and you will abide with Him forever!

As you prioritize your relationship with the Lord, you are going from glory to glory. Each time you choose Him, every moment you enjoy His Presence and bless Him with yours, He conveys His beautiful intentions for your life. With every touch of God's glory, you're gaining a greater capacity to radiate Christ.

As you abide in this heavenly awareness, the Holy One expands inside of you. Strength infuses you until you scarcely remember your reasons for resisting this royal calling. You are becoming increasingly capable of co-reigning with Him. Every aspect of who you are is transforming. Walking in power, anointing, love, and humble compassion is becoming second nature as His Spirit dispenses through you. You are the resting place of God. He has made His home in you.

My Heart's Response

Lord, I'm embracing this mystery—the Holy of Holies has become my home. And this vessel, once dark and sinful, has become Yours. You have made me whole; beautiful, radiant, powerful. Our union makes my heart sing. Thank You for choosing me, for intertwining Your nature into mine so that I look and sound just like You.

Now, I'm going to rest and enjoy our relationship. I'll live in the security of Your Presence, and find strength and guidance in this place I call home. I'll wait and listen as You instruct me, and I will boldly obey. I'm not afraid anymore because Your promise to never leave or forsake me is becoming a reality.

Every day, I will notice truth piercing my heart, deeper and deeper until it vibrates through every cell. I can be all You've created me to be because we are one. You're in me and You're not going anywhere!

Day 83

Remember Who You Are

Now it's time to be made new by every revelation that's been given to you. And to be transformed as you embrace the glorious Christ-within as your new life and live in union with him!

Ephesians 4:23-24 TPT

All that Jesus is, you are. Jesus Christ within you, His glory inside of you, is the very core of your design. The Holy Spirit of God is in the center of your spirit. This mingling of His Spirit and yours has recreated you. You are an entirely new being who is one spirit with the Lord.

All that He is, you are. You are love. You are glorious, purified, whole, peaceful, joyful, and wise. You are a spirit being, made to manifest the perfection, beauty, brilliance, and power of who God is. You are a living miracle, a mystery that is meant to be embraced before it can be fully understood!

Right now, become aware of every thought that's contrary to who Jesus says you are, to how much He loves you, and how powerful you are because of the One who resides within you. It's time to see yourself the way He sees you, and to agree with your Creator, to love yourself with tender acceptance and grace, to live with enthusiasm, joyfully anticipating the unfolding revelation of how powerful and glorious you are because of Him.

Jesus wants you to enjoy your life. He longs for you to let go and get to know His perfect, unfailing love. As you rest and live in the continual experience of Christ within you, you will become completely secure.

My Heart's Response

Jesus, thank You for moving in the depths of my being, and filling my heart with love and truth. Right now, I yield every thought that is contrary to who You say I am. Thank You for exposing areas of low self-esteem and self-worth, and connecting my heart to the wonder of my identity in You.

Your grace is leading me into truth. Your uncreated Spirit resides within me, equipping me to believe when my mind tries to get in the way. I'm being transformed by the revelations I embrace, so I embrace them wholeheartedly and without reservation. I'm soaking them in and letting them become a part of me. I am a new creation—a beautiful reflection of a holy God. Your nature, perfect and complete in every way, is mine. I am who You say I am.

Day 84

Lean Into His Strength

I am convinced that my God will fully satisfy every need you have, for I have seen the abundant riches of glory revealed to me through Jesus Christ!

Philippians 4:19 TPT

As I prayed into this scripture for us, I saw Jesus wrapping His arms around you. He drew you into His embrace. As you leaned in close, your head resting against His chest, you leaned into His strength. The strength of Almighty God infused every part of your soul that needed what only He could give.

This is a prophetic picture of Jesus' desire. Let your heart respond to His intention for you and lean into Him. Take a deep breath and receive fresh peace, comfort, and strength. He is pouring into you, calming the internal storms of stress, insecurity, and fear. Let them go. See each one melting into His love and dissolving as they touch His glory.

Any area of your soul that's overwhelmed or stuck in an emotional reaction or trigger is being soothed by His grace. Give each stressor to the Lord, and in exchange, He'll give you the ability to see the trials through the eyes of light, truth, and unquenchable faith.

His healing love makes everything look different. Perfect love shines the light that leads you out of obscurity. Lean into Jesus, sinking deep into His embrace, and He will radically transform every part of your existence. Jesus is strengthening you and comforting you. This is His promise for you today.

My Heart's Response

Yes, Lord, I'm leaning into You. Wrap me in Your arms and hold me tight until Your love obliterates every fear. Strengthen me. Whisper those words of truth that remind me that I am never alone, never too far gone, or too disillusioned to be rescued by You.

I can see now that when I feel like I'm sinking into a pit of despair, I'm in the perfect position to be carried by You. And when I'm entirely at rest in Your big, strong arms, completely yielded, trusting in Your strength and not my own, refreshing comes.

Thank You for Your overwhelming love. Thank You for this mercy that picks me up time after time and sets me on my feet again. You care for me more than my mind can comprehend. And now, I'm looking You in the eyes and drawing from Your strength. I can say that I am convinced that You will fully satisfy every need that I have.

Day 85

The Power of Love

A Prophetic Word

The time will come when all the earth is filled, as the waters fill the sea,
with an awareness of the glory of the Lord.
Habakkuk 2:14 TLB

One day, Jesus showed me the earth framed with a pyramid-like structure. I knew this pyramid had framed the reality and narrative of the planet quite extensively. But as I watched, the light of Jesus engulfed the structure, dissolving it entirely. It didn't just dismantle it, the light of Christ shone into the darkness and the darkness completely ceased to exist.

We are living in very difficult times, and in the end, the knowledge (or experience) of the glory of the Lord will cover the earth. But right now, God has hidden Himself in the midst of us. We are the ones filled with His glory-light, and we are about to express Him in an unprecedented way. As we submit to the Lord, we will release the light, sound, and Presence of our Creator and sovereign King.

Love is the key. Love is the brightness of His glory. When we live from the secret place, where we remain in His intoxicating, fear-dissolving love, we are transformed. As we constantly behold Him, living from our union with God, we will reflect Him into the earth. The world will look upon us and know that we are His because His love will shine from our lives. Agape love will ultimately cause darkness to cease to exist, and we will see that the earth and everything in it are His.

My Heart's Response

Jesus, kiss my heart awake so that this revelation will unfold within me. Leave no part of me untouched by the reality of Your love. My eyes are on You. My heart is fixed on the beauty of my King. Thank You that as I remain in Your Presence, You are dissolving any trace of darkness, doubt, and fear from my life.

You are drenching me in Your love and I will never be the same. I am becoming absolutely convinced of Your power inside of me. Your glory-light is streaming into every cell of my being. I am Your shining one, Your instrument of love on the earth.

Saturate me with this love until every part of me pours mercy, compassion, and glory. Lord, flow through me into this earth so that everyone I talk to feels the tangible reality of Your love. Love will cause Your Kingdom to be established everywhere I go.

Day 86

Centered and Stable

If we live in the Spirit, let us also walk in the Spirit.
Galatians 5:25 NKJV

Jesus is shattering restrictive thinking. He's expanding our understanding of the significance of our union with Him. He's blowing up our boxes and eliminating the limitations that have kept us from walking in the power of our oneness. As we tune into this reality, grace enables us to remain centered. Instead of bouncing back and forth between our soul and spirit, we're becoming stable, living from spirit to Spirit.

We're growing in confidence as the nature of Christ cascades into our nature. Our beliefs and actions display the divine strength of God because we're living from the core of this holy union. Now we will influence our culture and impact the people around us.

The Holy Spirit is increasing your capacity to receive this unfolding revelation—it is no longer I who lives, but Christ lives in me. This will be a personal, internal, transformational experience. This realignment will change you, and increase your influence and impact. Your prayers won't feel impotent, nor will your decrees be powerless. You will literally speak the heart and mind of God. As you remain in this spirit to Spirit connection, the world will grow dim, but your heavenly perspective will become clear. You'll be internally synchronized, living in tune with the heart of God.

My Heart's Response

Lord, thank You for unveiling the eyes of my understanding to sec our relationship more clearly. I know that we're one, but now the power of this mystery is going from my mind to my heart. I'm sitting under the wonder of this revelation and it's transforming me. Nothing matters more than knowing You and living in a way that honors You.

Your Presence within me stabilizes me so that no matter what comes, I'm grounded in truth. You're synchronizing my spirit to Your Spirit. I'm beginning to harmonize with the sounds of heaven, even while the world is loud and chaotic. My internal reality is becoming more real than what my natural eyes see. In trials, my soul finds its rest in You because I'm trusting Your love more than ever before.

My thoughts, desires, my whole world, is centered around You now. I'm living in the light of Your truth, guided by Your Spirit. Confident in our union, distractions no longer block my view of You. Instead, they point me to You and serve to strengthen my desire to live centered and stable in You.

Day 87

You Are Coming Alive

The eyes of your understanding being enlightened;
that you may know what is the hope of His calling...
Ephesians 1:18 NKJV

We are a new creation. We are the Lord's. The divine nature of the uncreated God is the core substance of our being. The old Adamic nature no longer defines us, but Christ's divine nature in us has transformed us into His image. Our conscious awareness has been reset. The eyes of our understanding are being enlightened, and we're becoming secure in who we are in Him. We are those whose beings are intertwined with Love Himself.

Before the foundation of the earth, the Lord preordained this holy shift in your life. He knew that the reality of your identity would come alive in your heart at this time and that you would begin to walk in a new way. You are becoming His confident bride, His mature son. It doesn't matter how unqualified you might feel. You are fully known and totally accepted by the Most Holy One. His love absorbed your failures, and you are radiant and perfectly loved.

This is the truth of heaven. This is what heaven is saying. It's time to abide in God's love and bear fruit for His Kingdom. This has always been the intention of God, and the Holy Spirit is invested in bringing forth the Father's purpose. Your life, overflowing with the glory of God, has always been the Godhead's plan. This is your time to rise and display His splendor.

My Heart's Response

Jesus, I am coming forth now, full of Your radiance. I celebrate what You've done so that I can live in the power of our oneness. It's only by Your grace that I can stand in my identity. I'm not the same person I once was. I'm not tossed around by every wind of adversity. You have empowered me. You have renewed me, and words fall short in expressing my gratitude.

My desires, my choices, and my walk are being perfected. My words and my thoughts flow from the wisdom and truth of Your Spirit in me. Your light and truth are guiding my decisions and my every step. The knowledge of the Holy One has rewired my thinking, and I'm in awe of how differently I see things now.

Lord, have Your way in me. Inundate me with Your glory until it radiates through every cell. I am becoming conscious of Your life in me, and this incredible awareness is becoming my everyday reality.

Day 88

Infused With Faith

Jesus replied, "Let the faith of God be in you!
Mark 11:22 TPT

Jesus wants our hearts to be at rest. He wants us to be confident, trusting in His love with one hundred percent immovable faith; faith that is powered by Him when we feel we have none of our own. Today, Jesus is encouraging our hearts. He's reminding us that He will manifest Himself in every single challenge or place of disillusionment. The testimony of His goodness will increase around the earth, and He will be glorified by how He turns every situation around for good. Take heart; God is redeeming your circumstances.

Everything we see in the Gospels is how Jesus is now. He is the same yesterday, today, and forever. He healed the sick, raised the dead, cleansed the lepers, and cast out demons. That's what He does. When the divine touches the natural, everything comes into Kingdom order. Light obliterates the darkness simply by shining, and nothing shines brighter than Jesus.

He is the glorious One. Jesus is our Healer, Comforter, and Friend. He is our hope, our light, and our entire world. And right now, He is pouring out grace for us to live in a level of faith that is unprecedented in our lives. We're receiving grace to help in time of need. We're becoming secure in Him, able to trust His love like never before. I decree that this will be your experience today.

My Heart's Response

Jesus, thank You for igniting my heart with fresh faith—Your faith. You are establishing me in truth so that the lies of the enemy do not entice me. Holy Spirit, thank You for enabling me to believe things that I once considered impossible. Now I see that nothing is impossible with You. You are working all things together for my good.

Nothing in my life is outside of Your control. So, I let go and relinquish my need to fix what I've tried to fix many times before. Instead, I'll rest in Your faithfulness and gaze upon Your face. Nothing stirs my faith like one glance of Your eyes. You are faithful even when my faith has been shaken.

Spirit, soul, and body, every part of me is wholly surrendered to You. Everything in my life is under the realm of Your authority. You're watching over Your word to perform it. You are not a man that You should lie, and your faithfulness endures forever.

Day 89

God's Got This

So we are convinced that every detail of our lives is continually woven together for good, for we are his lovers who have been called to fulfill his designed purpose.

Romans 8:28 TPT

I encourage you to read that verse again with your spirit. No matter how you feel, how out of control things in the world may seem, the promises of God are true. The intention of His heart is that you would unite your faith with this powerful truth: every single detail of your life is continually woven together to fit into God's perfect plan. So, even if you can't make sense of things right now, you can lean into this truth. You can lean into the faithfulness of who God is. You can trust His character.

He is the Alpha and the Omega. He is the One who wraps up human history according to His will. He created a plan from A to Z and knows how to accomplish it in your life. He is the truth, He is the way and the life. He continually weaves together every single detail of your existence. God is molding situations into conformity by the counsel of His perfect wisdom. He's bringing forth His unfailing plans and purposes.

You don't have to struggle to do it in your strength. All He asks is that you take Him at His word and believe. This is His work in your life. His Holy Spirit resides within you, establishing you, and bringing you forth to be a perfect reflection of God in the earth. You are the counterpart of God forever, and He will never forsake you.

My Heart's Response

Lord, You are love, joy, peace, goodness, truth, and faithfulness. I find everything I need in You. Thank You for holding my life so tenderly, so wisely, so graciously. You know every detail of my life. Nothing is hidden from You. Nothing is outside of Your redemptive power. You're holding it all together, weaving Yourself into every strand of my existence.

My capacity to rest and believe Your words is increasing. As I wait for Your instructions, You're saturating and strengthening me with the power of Your Spirit. I'm coming forth now, fully convinced of Your love and faithfulness.

I offer You my greatest act of worship—to abide in Your Presence with all of my heart, to pour out my life as a living sacrifice, to be a dwelling place of Your mighty power, and to trust that You will fulfill Your purposes in my life.

Day 90

You'll Never Be the Same

Arise, my darling! Come quickly, my beloved. ...We will dance in the high place of the sky, yes, on the mountains of fragrant spice. Forever we shall be united as one!

Song of Songs 8:14 TPT

The Lord has revealed His heart for you in an incredible way. As you've opened yourself to receive, you have shifted. This season has been a holy moment, escorting you into another level of glory, another dimension of His love; a new understanding of the provision that is already yours. You can live in the light, no matter how dark the world is.

This is the message of the Ancient of Days to you—you've been set free so that you can fulfill the dreams of His heart. You are rising strong, confident in His love so that you never have to fear again. Every day, as you draw from His strength, grace, and love, you are changing. You're awakening to a truth so profound that it's altering your entire belief system and the way you live.

No weapon formed against you, no intention of evil can prosper against you. You belong to the King. You are one with the King! The enemy has done everything he can to keep you asleep, weighed down by the cares of this world. But Jesus says, "No more! Awake My bride! Stand firmly in My love, and it will cause you to run. You've tasted and seen that I am good. You've embraced these treasures of wisdom and pulled them into your heart, and I have seen. You will never be the same again!"

My Heart's Response

Jesus, thank You for flooding my spiritual eyes and ears with fresh grace, life, and strength. My heart has been unveiled, and I'm seeing and hearing more clearly than ever before. You have come, and You have set me free. I have shifted in a way I never knew was possible. I'm standing now, believing now.

I know that You are for me, in me, and have surrounded me. I understand that Your nature is mine. The foundation of Your Word has anchored my soul, illuminated my path, and given me wisdom. I am Your bride, Your treasure, Your delight. I am Yours and You are mine. I am ready to run with You to the mountain heights and shine Your light. And I am so confident in Your love that I can sing Your praise in the deepest valley nights. You are with me, and I will never be the same.

About the Authors

Liz Wright is an international best selling author, speaker, host of the Charisma Podcast show Live Your Best Life with Liz Wright, and Founder of the International Mentoring Community. Liz's life changed forever in 1995 with a physical visitation from Jesus Christ. Since that time, she has helped millions around the globe to know the heart of God and experience His life-transforming love for themselves. For more about Liz, see her website: lizwright.org

Gretchen Rodriguez has authored several devotionals alongside Brian Simmons to accompany The Passion Translation. Her heart burns with one main message: intimacy with Jesus and discovering the reality of his presence. She and her husband invested nine years as missionaries in Puerto Rico, along with their three daughters, and now make San Antonio, Texas, their home. For more about Gretchen, see her website: GretchenRodriguez.com.

Other Books by Liz Wright

Reflecting God: Spiritual Keys to Unlock the Supernatural You

"These words are alive and if you engage them, they will open your heart to new dimensions of the limitless life in Christ. Enjoy this priceless book!" Justin Abraham

A life utterly transformed by Christ's Spirit is the most exhilarating, fulfilling, powerful life we can ever imagine. It is God's dream for you to live this way, experiencing the reality of New Creation Life, every day. You are the revelation of Jesus on earth now. His reflection!

Ekklesia Rising: Visitations From Jesus Revealing the Truth & Power of Who We Really Are

"I truly believe that reading this book your life will never be the same. Every word is imbued with the Presence of Jesus and has been birthed through supernatural encounter." Wendy Alec.

You will become empowered to experience a level of freedom and peace you never thought possible. With a renewed security in the absolute love of God, you will be set free to live out of your authentic self and so begin to produce your highest purpose.

Liz Wright's books are available on Amazon in hard copy and Kindle.

Liz Wright International Mentoring Community (IMC)

The purpose of the IMC is to facilitate a **safe environment** where **like-minded** people at any stage of maturity can enter into a **deeper experience** of Jesus.

What's included:

- Friday Zoom call with Liz and amazing guest speakers
- Private, members-only Facebook group
- Send in your questions and prayer requests
- Spiritual Thought for the Day videos
- Behind the Scenes clips of Live Your Best Life
- Access the Member Portal with ALL past video content including Q&A videos and Facebook Live prayer sessions
- Free digital copy of Reflecting God
- Plus gifts and surprises along the way!

Learn more on lizwright.org

E-courses & Soaking Audios

Secrets of the Secret Place

An 8 session series with Liz, activating you into the simple enjoyment and overcoming power of a life beholding the face of Jesus.

Ekklesia Rising

In this 4 week course, break free from bondage and be activated into a level of peace and liberty that you may have never thought was possible! Living insecure and without the awareness of Jesus' Presence will become a distant memory.

View e-courses at courses.lizwright.org

Made in the USA
Monee, IL
06 February 2022

514e2f70-3191-4280-becb-59ec2fa5f9bbR01